Making Our Schools the Best in the World

Other Books by M. Scott Norton

The Principal as a Learning-Leader: Motivating Students by Emphasizing Achievement

Competency-Based Leadership: A Guide for High Performance in the Role of the School Principal

Teachers with the Magic: Great Teachers Change Students' Lives

The Changing Landscape of School Leadership: Recalibrating the School Principalship

The Legal World of the School Principal: What Leaders Need to Know about School Law

Guiding Curriculum Development: The Need to Return to Local Control

Guiding the Human Resources Function in Education: New Issues, New Needs

A Guide for Educational Policy Governance: Effective Leadership for Policy Development

Dealing with Change: The Effects of Organizational Development on Contemporary Practices

The White House and Education through the Years: U.S. Presidents' Views and Significant Education Contributions

Improving Education in a World of Politics: Recommendations and Strategies for Effective Political Participation

Making Our Schools the Best in the World

Reimagining Education Outside the Proverbial Box

M. Scott Norton

ROWMAN & LITTLEFIELD
Lanham • Boulder • New York • London

Published by Rowman & Littlefield
An imprint of The Rowman & Littlefield Publishing Group, Inc.
4501 Forbes Boulevard, Suite 200, Lanham, Maryland 20706
www.rowman.com

6 Tinworth Street, London SE11 5AL, United Kingdom

Copyright © 2019 by M. Scott Norton

All rights reserved. No part of this book may be reproduced in any form or by any electronic or mechanical means, including information storage and retrieval systems, without written permission from the publisher, except by a reviewer who may quote passages in a review.

British Library Cataloguing in Publication Information Available

Library of Congress Cataloging-in-Publication Data Available

ISBN: 978-1-4758-4702-4 (cloth : alk. paper)
ISBN: 978-1-4758-4703-1 (pbk. : alk. paper)
ISBN: 978-1-4758-4704-8 (electronic)

∞™ The paper used in this publication meets the minimum requirements of American National Standard for Information Sciences—Permanence of Paper for Printed Library Materials, ANSI/NISO Z39.48–1992.

Printed in the United States of America

Contents

Preface		vii
1	Public School Education in America: Patchwork or a Complete Makeover?	1
2	Reimagining the Failing Factors of Public School Education	31
3	Social Issues and the Importance of Public Education for Dealing with Them	63
4	Public School Education as the Best of All Worlds	85
About the Author		115

Preface

Why This Book Was Written

For every educational program proposal or intervention implemented, there invariably is a counterresponse opposing the matter. For every article contending that education in America is failing, there is an opposing article contending that America's education is among the world's best. This book, *Education as the Best of All Worlds*, is based on a reimagination of education and what is needed to make public education the best of all worlds. Attention centers on what must be done to eliminate present educational restraints and dream the impossible dreams that indeed serve to place education in its desired position of the best of all worlds. An invading theme centers on what must be done to meet the educational goals required to maintain our democratic form of government, to provide the knowledge and skills required for our free enterprise system, and to give each individual, as Lincoln said, "an unfettered start and fair chance in the race of life."

Current educational programs are unsatisfactory in all too many school districts. Teacher turnover is such that attempts to bring stability into the programs are difficult at best. Teachers are underpaid, and the ability to attract needed talent into the profession is increasingly problematic. Many persons believe that student dropout rates are being increased due to student apathy. If this contention is true, this result is directly opposite of student engagement that must be emphasized in teacher preparation programs. Both teacher preparation programs and administrative preparations programs are being questioned. Administrator turnover has constantly increased over the past few decades. Virtually every social issue facing the nation has been viewed as a problem that must be addressed through effective programs of education.

School board policy development, for the most part, has been turned over to outside agencies such as state associations of school boards. As a result, local control of public education has waned; local control of education has been decreased in many school districts. Disconnects between and among teachers' groups and the local school district administration and the loss of confidence on the part of parents have been voiced and become troublesome.

The old cliché, "outside the box," represents major changes and needed reimagination of what education in our country must do to remain viable. We refrain from making simple statements such as "education needs more money" or "we need to improve our administrator preparation programs"; rather, the book sets forth the proverbial "box" strategies that represent major changes in several present models of education programming. No one has a magic wand to make such improvements just happen. What is needed is revolutionary program interventions that result in what all thinking citizens in America seek, a public school education program that is the best of all worlds.

How This Book Is Organized

The contents of the book are presented in four relevant chapters. Each chapter includes a primary goal, a reader-friendly style, reader engagement activities, snapshots of successful education programming, discussion questions, and support references. Book chapters focus on the reimagination of educational programing related to educational economics, social issues, personnel preparation, school board member requirements, teacher preparation, educational funding, and related changes in educational governance.

Chapter 1 of the book is designed to establish the groundwork and rationale for needed major changes in governance and personnel practices in education. Current educational programs and practices that are not working effectively are identified along with others that have served education advantageously over the years.

In chapter 2, the current personnel preparation programs for teachers and school administrators are discussed in depth with recommendations that must be implemented to improve the attraction of education as a professional interest on the part of the most talented personnel. Their retention in the profession is discussed as being of paramount importance for reaching the quality of being best. The importance of the economics of education and what has to be done to finance quality programs of student learning has been discussed. A "best of all worlds" education program that parallels other professional careers in medicine, engineering, business, law, and others must not only attract the best but compensate the best to retain them on the job.

Chapter 3 centers on the social issues that face the nation and the extent to which education is responsible for dealing with such matters. Such programming cannot be achieved without a new concept of school programming that serves above and beyond only academic learning in math and science.

Chapter 4 centers on the reimagination of preparation and continuous learning changes for aspiring and practicing educational personnel. Major changes in the preparation of teachers and administrators are recommended along with other revolutionary interventions that are needed to change the image of public schools from average to high quality—the best of all worlds.

Special features of the book include the use of "thought exercises," light-bulb experiences, discussion questions, and quizzes to increase the reader's engagement in the book's content and to foster interest in extended learning. Case studies, post-chapter quizzes, and discussion questions are included in an effort to meet this objective.

Who Would Be Most Interested in Purchasing This Book?

All educational personnel would find that the book is focused on important innovations that must be given serious consideration if education is to overcome its present reputation as a failing entity. Teachers, administrators, and school boards are well aware that the economic, social, and program aspects of public schools are resulting in growing nonsupport. This book sets forth a reimagination of aims and strategies needed to help education to reverse its downfall. The citizenry in general has lost confidence in America's schooling practices. They too would be interested readers of this book.

Although the book sets forth new recommendations for the preparation programs for aspiring teachers and administrators, each of these groups would benefit a great deal by knowing what possibilities can be reached with their serious thinking and personal support. The book should be in the professional libraries of both teachers and administrators. When educational professionals are asked about the efficacy of their personal preparation program, commonly they express that they had hopes for more relevant and workable educational experiences that did not take place. The book emphasizes ways in which preparation must be reimagined.

A Final Thought

The work is not viewed as being just another educational reform book. Rather, it is a far-reaching attempt to reverse current educational programs that have become ineffective and to innovate new revolutionary changes that are essential for leading America's education toward being the best of all worlds.

Chapter 1

Public School Education in America
Patchwork or a Complete Makeover?

Primary chapter goal: To examine the wide division of views relative to the current effectiveness of public school education in America and the major reasons why educational reforms seldom result in long-term improvements, wide public acceptance, or equity for learners nationwide.

In an article set forth by McSpadden (2015), the primary contention was that public schools in America are doing very well. In fact, in schools with less than 25 percent poverty rates, American children scored higher in reading than any children in other countries. Yet, in 2014, reports indicated that latest international ratings of education in sixty-five countries showed that public schools in America are in a freefall (Fedewa 2014); the United States ranked twenty-ninth in education in the world.

A few years ago, Sager (2013) contended that the educational system in the United States is in dire trouble and there seemed to be little real hope of effective reform in the near future. He further stated that the educational system has been in a state of decline for decades. Yet, on the other hand, Rampell (2014) cited research that supported the fact that public education is getting better, not worse.

A more recent reference supported public schools and pointed out that public education has gotten a bad rap. Chen (2018) supported Rampell's foregoing contention by pointing out several advantages of public schools including factors such as cost, diversity, academic opportunities, extracurricular opportunities, services, teacher qualifications, and other positive factors.

Another source set forth the wide claim that today's schools are better than at any point in the past (Schneider 2016). This writer described several indicators that reveal slow but steady improvement in education across many generations. Schneider astutely closes his argument for providing a first-rate public education for every child in America in the paragraph that follows (Schneider 2016).

The evolution of America's school system has been slow. But providing a first-rate public education to every child in the country is a monumental task. Today, 50 million U.S. students attend roughly 100,000 schools and are educated by over 3 million teachers. The scale alone is overwhelming. And the aim of schooling is equally ambitious. Educators are not just designing gadgets or building websites. At this phenomenal scale, they are trying to make people—a fantastically difficult task for which there is no quick fix. No simple solution. No "hack."

Can policy leaders and stakeholders accelerate the pace of development? Probably. Can the schools do more to realize national ideals around equity and inclusion? Without question. But none of these aims will be achieved by ripping the system apart. That's a ruinous fiction. The struggle to create great schools for all young people demands swift justice and steady effort, not melodrama and magical thinking (8–9).

NOT MELODRAMA AND MAGICAL THINKING

The foregoing positions relative to the status of public education, for the most part, are based on personal opinions and perspectives. But is there reliable and valid evidence that reveals the true status of public education in America? This chapter centers on the status of public education as revealed in official status reports of major educational organizations, agencies of the states, and federal governments and other highly reliable sources.

In the following sections of this chapter, study results rather than public opinions of the pluses and minuses of education are reported. If high-quality school programs can be authenticated, leaders in education can capitalize on such findings. If studies can ferret out what factors are inhibiting public education in America, this information gives leaders a basis for reimagining education with a positive perspective in mind for the future. This chapter centers on six major charges against public education that commonly accompany claims of education's failures and then sets forth five major support factors that are claimed as public education's successes. Identification of positive and negative perspectives of public education is considered but recommended changes are specifically addressed. Reimagining educational changes is discussed in depth in chapters 2, 3, and 4.

CRITICAL FAILURES OF PUBLIC EDUCATION

Among the myriad of criticisms of public education are the following *inhibiting factors* commonly set forth as failures of public education: (1) lack of financial support including low teachers' salaries; (2) inequities in public school programs across the states; (3) the widening control of education by the states and federal government agencies; (4) the lack of highly qualified teachers and administrator personnel; (5) poor student academic performance that is identified in the list of major factors that result in the failure of public schools; and (6) the "disorganization of schools" including an excessive number of school administrators with overlapping functions, administrative mismanagement, too many inefficient school districts that should be consolidated, and far too many curricular subjects consuming high percentages of the school's budget.

Although the lack of valid and reliable research evidence is not commonly mentioned as an inhibitor of public school success, we contend that it indeed is a missing activity in education. We have taken the factor of "author's privilege" and added it to the list of public school inhibiting factors. Give a moment's thought to the matter of research in educational practices. Can you name a school district that has a quality education research program in operation?

We are not looking at educational research as being the statistical unit for the school district—one in which the student enrollment figures and academic testing programs are reported. Rather, we view the school district's research unit to be one that focuses on the ongoing dissemination of educational research relative to planned pilot programs, active classroom research findings, program findings on topics of educational significance completed by other school districts or agencies, and related research in cooperation with teachers in determining such topics as the learning styles of students in the school.

Each of the inhibiting factors of education is discussed in the following sections of this chapter. Following that, chapters 2, 3, and 4 focus on the revolutionary changes that must be implemented to overcome these major inhibitors. We begin by discussing the six major inhibitors of public school education as reported within the literature.

MAJOR FACTORS INHIBITING PUBLIC SCHOOL QUALITY

Inhibitor #1
Inadequate Financial Support

Former U.S. president, Richard Nixon, declared that just putting more money into current educational programs will not assure improvements in public education. The contention does hold considerable truth. Giving more money to low-performing school personnel certainly does not assure that teachers' performance will improve. However, new money for attracting highly knowledgeable and qualified personnel into education is a much different story. Research evidence has been shown to support the finding that many persons with high intelligence scores are not entering the teaching profession. When they do enter the profession, a large percentage of these talented persons leave teaching after only one year.

Klein (2011) was straightforward in his contentions for fixing the present education compensation schemes. We paraphrase his comments regarding what should be done to enable the system to meet its financial needs. Rather than to pay for longevity and lifetime benefits, Klein contends that we must reward excellence. To do so, automatic raises and promises of large lifetime benefits would have to be eliminated. The enormous amounts of money saved could be devoted to performance pay, difficult teaching assignment incentives, and successful recruiting in those subject areas where shortage is in evidence.

In addition, Klein speaks of frontloading compensation whereby new teachers could receive as much as $80,000 within four years of service. Think of how such a provision would serve to attract and retain new highly qualified teacher personnel. The loss of 20 percent to 30 percent of teachers new to the profession would lessen considerably. Education personnel would receive this frontloading of compensation in the early years of their educational experience. They would not have to wait for twenty-five years or more to "cash in" on the present back-loaded structure. In brief, Klein proposed eliminating the lifetime, defined pensions, monetizing the savings, and then paying it to teachers in their early years. A second alternative was suggested by Rhee (2011) that centered on a merit plan whereby teachers could earn higher salaries during their early entry into teaching. We support this "out of the proverbial box" thinking.

The old adage that individuals do not enter teaching for the money, but they do so for the love of children, is flawed. Contemporary teacher strikes, such as the *RedforEd 2018* strikes in Arizona, are a case in point. The whole purpose of the 2018 Arizona teacher strike was that of salary increases. The state's agreement to increase teachers' salaries 20 percent by 2020 served to resolve the problem for the meantime. Yet, additional teacher demands were soon to follow.

There is sufficient evidence to show that increasingly the classroom teacher is responsible for paying for needed classroom instructional materials. As one teacher pointed out, to do the job that she wants to do, she spends personal funds in the amount that commonly equals the raise that she received for the school year. There appears to be no secret regarding the importance of funding for recruiting and retaining highly talented teacher personnel. Most every "expert" simply says, pay teachers what the market demands, provide them with benefits that are competitive, and create a work environment in which they can derive genuine professional satisfaction.

Such provisions call for the discontinuance of the single salary schedule whereby all teachers with the same degree and years of experience receive the same compensation regardless of the supply and demand principle or differences in professional job performance. Such obvious solutions are not always easy to implement. Educational finance is among the most difficult inhibitors of quality public school education; getting more money for education is viewed by many authorities as the number one problem being encountered.

Sager (2013) contends that in the face of shortfalls and decreased tax revenues, many school systems in the nation have cut their educational programs. Such cuts result in lasting damages to the education of students. Financial cuts are implemented at the expense of educational quality and result in the contention that America's schools are failing. Lack of funding also leads to the unfortunate practices of cutting programs of learning, reduction of the school year, and in some cases, reducing the school week from five days to four. Those parties that contend that money is not the cause of failing education in America are failing themselves to recognize that cuts in financial support mean cuts in student learning. Recommended solutions to school failure and finances are presented in chapter 2.

Inhibitor #2
Educational Inequities across States and School Districts

The Question: Does Variation in Per-Pupil Spending
Explain Most of the Variations in School Quality?

For the most part, public school education is viewed as a state responsibility. Within our fifty states, education equity differs widely. In fact, the quality of public education within any one state differs within the many school districts that commonly exist. Richie Bernardo, writing for *WalletHub* (2018), reported on a fifty-state study that compared the quality of public education in the fifty states on twenty-one key measures. Although the report did come up with several measures of education quality, unfortunately no attention apparently was given to the extent to which the highest rated states financially supported public education. That report asked the question, "Does variation in per-pupil spending explain most of the variation in school quality?" but did not offer an answer.

We referred to the *WalletHub* study of public school quality rankings, which gave the state of Massachusetts the highest quality ranking with the states of New Jersey, Connecticut, New Hampshire, and Vermont next in order of best public schools. The lowest-quality public schools were in New Mexico,

Table 1.1. Highest and Lowest Quality School Ratings & Per-Pupil Financial Support

High School Quality State Rankings	Per-Pupil Spending ($)
1st Massachusetts	15,592
2nd New Jersey	18,235
3rd Connecticut	18,377
4th New Hampshire	14,697
5th Vermont	18,039

Low School Quality State Rankings	Per-Pupil Spending ($)
50th New Mexico	9,792
42nd Mississippi	8,456
48th Arizona	7,485
47th Alaska	20,172
46th West Virginia	11,359

Mississippi, Arizona, Alaska, and West Virginia. Just how do these state ratings compare with per-pupil expenditures for public education? In a completely different report published by *Room 41* of Oregon's Concordia University (2018), the state monetary support per pupil shown in table 1.1 was determined.

Other states with per-pupil spending support of $14,697 or more were the states of New Hampshire with $14,697, New York with a quality ranking of twentieth and per-pupil support of $21,206, Pennsylvania with a quality ranking of twenty-eight and per-pupil support of $14,717, Rhode Island with a quality ranking of twenty-first and per-pupil support of $15,179, and Wyoming with a quality rating of eighteenth and per-pupil support of $16,056.

We note, once again, that the two study reports, one for state education quality and the other for per-pupil spending support, were two separate and distinct reports. The comparative information relative to state education quality and state spending is interesting and does reveal some evidence for answering the question posed at the outset of this section: Does variation in per-pupil spending explain most of the variations in school quality? We contend that financial support does provide some insight for answering the question. However, Alaska with its high school per-pupil spending of $20,172 and New York with per-pupil spending of $21,206 ranked forty-second and twentieth for school quality, respectively. Authorities tend to view these two states as special cases due to several factors such as population differences, territorial differences, professional personnel issues, and other student clientele differences that must be attended in these states.

A Lightbulb Experience

Kyle Jaeger (2015) published an "inequalities article" that is pertinent to our consideration of property valuations and educational tax support. Jaeger notes that half of the country's property value comes from only the five states of California, New York, Florida, Texas, and Pennsylvania, respectively. Furthermore, income inequality is a growing problem in America and as the gap between the rich and poor continues to widen, disparities between property values per state will also increase over time.

As Jaeger points out clearly, only four states are worth more than New York City, property-wise, one of which is New York State. It tends to open one's eyes to the matter of inequity when it is noted that some Manhattan neighborhoods on the east upper side, which occupy less than one square mile, have an outstanding $96 billion of housing value. This fact, according to Jaeger, places it above Staten Island and the Bronx, as well as above the six other states of New Hampshire, North Dakota, South Dakota, Vermont, Wyoming, and Alaska. As we are well aware, local public school support comes primarily from monies gained through property taxes.

Statistics relative to the financial status of the fifty states have shown that the ability to pay for education differs in a ratio from 6 to 1. That is, the richest states are six times more able to pay for educational services than the poorest states. A related note focuses on the fact that just given equal amounts of monetary support to rich and poor school communities does nothing to adjust the inequities that exist. For example, if $a < b$ then $a + c < b + c$, meaning that if school district "a" has less property valuation for school purposes than school district "b," then just giving the same school monetary support to each school district does not improve the inequity that exists.

Inhibitor #3
Decreasing Local Control of Public Education

The U.S. Constitution makes no mention of education but the Tenth Amendment to the Constitution does give the responsibilities not set forth in the constitution to the states and its people. Thus, education commonly has been viewed as a federal concern, state responsibility, and local function. As a local function, district school boards have the primary responsibility of providing policies to guide the actions of those to whom they delegate administrative authority. The formulation and adoption of these written policies constitute the primary method by which the board of education exercises its leadership in the operation of the school system (Norton 2017).

School board policy development, adoption, and implementation have several special benefits for the local school system because (1) the quality of teaching and learning effectiveness can be improved because the school is administered by the individuals and boards that are most knowledgeable about the school-community and its students' interests and needs; (2) the school purposes and policy decisions are determined by representative school board members and the governance process includes a close working relationship with members of the school staff and community; (3) the external control is substantially reduced, which facilitates positive decision making and implementation of meaningful administrative regulations that can be readily applied to programs for student learning; and (4) local development, adoption, and implementation of school policy provide an important opportunity for the involvement of local school personnel and representative school-community members to participate in the process. Thus, the adopted policies become the personal product of not only the school board but also the teachers, parents, and other persons who served in their development.

Negative effects on public school quality are also found in other external interventions by federal and state agencies and other state and national associations. The federal government has found its program priorities in various program activities over the years. Vocational education, agricultural programs, physical education interventions, math, science, special student needs programs, foreign language requirements, and other curricular subjects have found their way into public school programs over the years by federal authorities. Teaching content and methodology were required by federal agencies under the Common Core mandates accompanied by a major increase in student testing measures that served to control public school program operations. Each mandated program was accompanied by federal monies that controlled local curricular operations.

In most every state, school board policies are developed by the state's school board association. Thus, in most every state, every school district has the same policies and administrative regulations using the alpha system for codification purposes. In the foregoing chapter discussion of the benefits of effective school governance policies, we underscored the importance of local school district involvement in the policy development process. When a state's school board association develops the policies for the school district, local control of the school's program is severely threatened and the importance of participative involvement in the process is disregarded. As a result, a school district's policy manuals lie dormant on shelves in teachers' classrooms gathering dust.

Policy control is the chief control operant of any school board. When this responsibility is given up by the local school board, external forces tend to intervene in policy matters and local control is jeopardized. Policy has several specific characteristics. First and foremost, policy sets forth the purposes that the school programs are to achieve. They are related to a general area of major importance to the school system and citizenry. A policy is a broad statement that allows for freedom of interpretation and execution. It is equivalent to legislation and commonly is applicable over long periods of time. Policies are the primary responsibility of the school board and can only be adopted by the school board. A policy serves to answer the question, "What to do?"

When local school board control is weakened, external forces tend to enter into the business of the school. Local school-community purposes of education give way to external mandates and curricular program requirements that must be implemented if certain external funds are to be appropriated. Of primary importance is the probable loss of internal school-community interest and support. Student interests and needs are determined by external forces as opposed to school-community members with the leadership of an informed and qualified school board membership.

Inhibitor #4
Poor Student Academic Performance

Criticism of public education programs and practices has been an ongoing practice in education history. For example, sixty years ago, James Bryant Conant published his best-selling book, *The American High School Today* (1959), which had major influence on educational reforms at the time. Among his reform statements were his recommendations to consolidate high schools into larger bodies for the purpose of extending curricular offerings, changing of teacher certification whereby independent bodies could no longer certify teachers, and he recommended the controversial practice of de facto segregation of students that segregated students in fact but not according to the requirements of law. Perhaps no other educational statement since has had the effect on education reform that Conant's book had in 1959. Yet, we still hear reform statements that include Conant's recommendations as set forth above.

Inhibitor #5
Inability to Attract and Retain Quality Teachers and Administrative Personnel

All teachers in America's public school classrooms are fully trained to lead a classroom, or are they? The answer is that they are not. Ricardo Cano of the *Arizona Republic* (2018b) reports that nearly 7,200 teaching certificates have been issued to teachers in Arizona who are not fully trained for teaching. In fact, since 2015, the number of Arizona teaching certificates issued to teachers who aren't fully trained has increased by more than 400 percent according to the state's Department of Education data as analyzed by Cano and the *Arizona Republic* newspaper personnel. The issuance of teaching certificates to teachers not fully trained for the position has continued to increase each year since 2015. With this record, what would be expected regarding student performance on standardized tests and general-education results?

The problem of attracting quality personnel into the teaching profession has been a problem historically. The problem of retaining their services is a related serious problem. The fact that teacher turnover commonly reaches 30 percent after only the first year of teaching is generally well known and accepted. After five years, teacher loss reaches 50 percent. That is, of the group of teachers that enter teaching for the first time, after five years 50 percent of this group have left the profession. We contend that both the recruitment of qualified teaching personnel and their retention are major problems; no organization can maintain stability with such high statistics of employee turnover.

Major changes in the way that professional teachers are recruited, assigned, developed, and compensated must be made in order for the stability problem to be reversed. A later chapter of the book deals with these needed major program and personnel changes. If not implemented, education most likely will continue to be viewed as failing. Educators themselves are overly conservative when it comes to "promoting" the early interests of children and youth in the professional field of education. School field trips, classroom helpers, student clubs, and other in-school activities might turn the attention of talented students toward a personal interest in teaching as a sought-after career.

Inhibitor #6
Flawed Organizational Procedures
and Mismanagement within School Districts

The following example, set forth on the opening page of this chapter, from the *Arizona Republic* (2018a), serves to underscore a major problem of public school failure. In the article, "State Will Take Over Murphy School District," the Arizona State Board of Education voted to appoint a receiver to oversee the district's operation among a $2.2 million spending deficit that publicly unraveled years of tension within the community and mismanagement in the district. It is beyond the scope of this chapter to discuss all of the issues and problems that surrounded the apparent "death" of this school district, but a number of problems related to financial woes, including disillusionment with district leadership, teacher/staff protests, angry parents, large classroom sizes, administrative resignations, loss of quality personnel, unfilled administrative positions, loss of school board members, and a variety of other dysfunctional operations within the school district were identified. But this is only one school district. No such difficulties are facing other school districts nationally.

During the gathering of ideas for this book, we visited schools and asked opinions of the personnel relative to school effectiveness. All too often we heard comments such as, "I've been an administrator in this school system for fifteen years and never been asked to serve on any system-wide committee or participated in the development of any major school policy" and "the school system is disengaged in that the central district office really does not know what we face at the local school level and we don't really know what the central staff is doing or thinking." Such statements make it clear that these school systems lack the qualities necessary for an effective learning culture to operate. We discuss the concept of organizational development (OD) in later chapters but note its purposes and importance in the following statement by Norton:

> When effectively implemented, OD fosters a school climate that promotes student achievement, increases positive collaboration among members of the school/school system, gains the commitment of personnel toward viewing change as an ongoing phenomena that requires planned strategies that lead to problem solutions, promotes creative thinking and the development of new knowledge and skills that enhance worker self-fulfillment, fosters an open climate that facilitates effective communication and resolutions of inevitable conflicts, and operates on the premise that schools are people and that the human factor looms important in the achievement of program goals. (2018, 11)

OD has been defined in a variety of different ways but commonly is viewed as "an effort to improve the effectiveness of all components of an organization using the knowledge of behavior science" (Gupta 2008, 1). OD encompasses four characteristics that serve to foster positive change: (1) Input: Preliminary planning. Diagnosing current production/achievement status, gathering from all sources within the organization, collecting and analyzing data of current results, preliminary procedures of action planning, implementing activities that serve toward *unfreezing behaviors* and procedures presently in place; (2) Transformation: Actions that center on new learning within the organization, steps that serve to gain the new knowledge and skills needed to achieve the changes needed within the organization. New learning serves to foster the confidence and acts as motivators for personnel engagement in the action plans; (3) Output: The realization of changes in worker behavior, evaluation and assessment of change, results through the use of purposeful data gathering. Both production and human behavior changes are evaluated and assessed. Successful results are put into place by *refreezing behaviors and procedures in place*; and (4) Feedback: The OD change model is not a one-time activity. Following each successful output change, a new cycle of change renewal is implemented (Norton 2018, 5–6).

MAJOR SUCCESS FACTORS OF PUBLIC EDUCATION: THE OTHER SIDE OF THE STORY

The *success factors* that are most commonly set forth in support of public education are the following: (1) the academic opportunities being provided by public education and its role of being a place where children can receive care, sustenance, safety, and the opportunity to learn; (2) education's availability/inclusiveness to all students including those with special needs; (3) the improvement of teacher preparation programs within institutions of higher education over the years; (4) the relative high percentage of high school graduates who enroll in college; and (5) the fact that education has produced a high level of social mobility and helped to create a shared culture that is essential to the maintenance of a democratic society (Kowal and Thomas 2002).

Success #1
Learning Opportunities in the Nation's Public Schools

Successful public schools are ones that have gained the confidence of the school-community by creating an environment for teaching and learning and the school principal and faculty have answered the key questions of: Why does our school exist? What is our purpose? What is our reason for being here? When each question is purposely explored, the answers fall on the concept that the school is for the provision of learning opportunities for all students inclusively; school leaders and staff are student advocates and as such center on opportunities that best reflect the individual interests and needs of each student. Learning opportunities are provided at the success level of each student. Student success widens the opportunity path for each individual.

By opportunities, we refer to the many opportunities that a public school education provides for growth and development. Such involvement provides the student more chances to do something different and better. As Eleanor Roosevelt said, "If you prepare yourself you will be able to grasp opportunity for broader experience when it appears." Opportunities to grow and develop occur in the academic arena but also are provided in a social context. Students are interacting with other students, teachers, and adults, as well as participating in athletics, clubs, and community events. Academic opportunities are provided in so many different professional, business, vocational, science, and civic areas, not dismissing the areas of the fine arts. In later chapters, we contend that the opportunities for personal participation in the profession of education should be promoted as well.

Success #2
Education's Inclusiveness for *All* Students

Inclusiveness represents one of the primary success factors of public education. Inclusiveness, whereby all students including those with special needs and/or disabilities are included in general-education facilities, was advanced by Madeleine Will, the former assistant secretary of education, in the late 1980s and early 1990s. The movement expanded into the belief that education should be ready to accept all students and a program be developed that meets the interests and needs of each individual. This concept differs from the concept of setting certain standards for each and every student to achieve; rather, learning was based on what is termed the success level for each student.

In addition, inclusion in public school education is founded on a commitment to several basic principles: (1) every student is viewed as important for having the capacity to help achieve the purposes that the school has set forth; (2) every student is shown value and respect; (3) and the school has developed an environment where students grow and development in a learning culture, and (4) every child is accepted and has a personal sense of belonging.

Federal legislation has been passed to assure that a student is placed in the least restricted environment for learning. Such a provision does not give the parents or students the authority to determine what is best for the student's placement; as long as the classroom in which the student is placed allows for personal improvement, the courts have ruled that such placement meets the requirements of the law. The concept certainly represents one of the success factors of public education. Inclusiveness is discussed additionally in later chapters of the book.

Success #3
Improved Teacher Education Programs across Institutions of Higher Eduction

Teacher training has advanced from the institution of *teacher institutes* operated by county superintendents in the nineteenth century. Graduation from high school and attendance at a summer teacher institute commonly satisfied the preparation requirements for elementary school teachers. Over the years, normal schools that centered on two years of preparation for teachers gave way to four-year college training in departments of education. Even though teachers in most every state are now required to have a four-year degree in education with state licensure in teaching, the demand for classroom teachers has introduced other ways and means for being allowed to serve in the classroom.

In addition, most every state has accompanying requirements for practicing teachers to earn college credits in appropriate subject-matter courses for renewal of the teacher's license. A common practice today, however, is for a teacher to gain credits by pursuing a master's degree. Such a step not only tends to satisfy license requirements but also results in moving upward on the salary schedule. The major criticism of this practice, however, is that it does not serve to improve the teacher's classroom performance in that, all too often, his or her work has been done in the area of administrative supervision.

Although education success entry #3 does focus on teacher preparation and improvement, both teacher and administrative preparation are being greatly criticized today. That is, although teacher preparation has improved greatly over the years, teacher performance is viewed as being unsatisfactory by many critics. This topic is discussed in depth in a later chapter of the book.

Success #4
A Relative High Number of High School Graduates Entering College

Statistics concerning the percentage of high school graduates who enter college have been relatively consistent in recent years, although reported statistics do differ. In the year 2013, 66.2 percent of high school graduates enrolled in college. Three years later in 2016, the statistic rose to 69.7 percent or 3.5 percent higher. We view that as a success statistic for public schools.

After all, some graduates enroll in vocational education programs, join some branch of the military service, or enter some other positive career in the world of work.

We are well aware of the critical facts that college dropout rates are high and that too many universities report that, according to the results of the respected ACT (American College Test), students come to them from the public schools unprepared for college. As reported by *NBC News* (Chuck 2015), just over half of all college students actually graduate.

In spite of the less than positive information reported in the foregoing section, we retain the factor of high school graduates entering college as a success factor for public schools. The consideration of having two-thirds of the public school graduates enrolling in college, in our view, establishes the fact that the large majority of students have learned the value of education and have been motivated to try to fulfill this important objective. As one interviewee said to us, "Even though I did not make it through college, I have learned the importance of supporting my kids in that pursuit." We discuss the topic of educating students about the education profession in later chapters of the book.

Success #5
The Production of Social Mobility and Shared Culture: Nurturing Democracy and Enhancing Potential for Adult Success

The importance of public education for the retention of a democratic society has been emphasized by our national presidents from the time of our first national president, George Washington, in 1779. As he commented in his welfare address to the nation, "The more homogeneous our Citizens can be made in these particulars, the greater will be our prospect of permanent union; and primary object of such a national institution should be the education of our youth in the science of *government*." Ulysses S. Grant stated that "the free school is the promoter of that intelligence which is to preserve us as a nation." As stated by Lyndon B. Johnson, "From the very beginning of our nation, we have felt a fierce commitment to the idea of education for everyone. It fixed itself into our democratic creed." And as stated by President Obama, "Our public education system is the key to opportunity for millions of children . . . It needs to be the best in the world."

Give thought to the social relationships that students experience in grades K–12. Yes, bullying, disobedience, and other uncivil behavior occur all too often in our schools. But as noted by Organization for Economic Cooperation and Development (OECD 2016), these negatives should serve as learning experiences for the parties involved. Social activities, cooperative relationships, and leadership opportunities, along with both winnings and losses, are most often experienced in the public school environment. Lessons of courtesy, for example, are common in a school environment but are not always available in the home.

We were told the story of one teacher who taught senior class members how to introduce themselves or a friend to their parents or to some other person of renown—a seemingly unimportant courtesy but one of needed civility. Is it, "Mother, I would like you to meet my friend Janice?" Or is it, "Janice, I would like you to meet my mother?" Or is it, "Grandmother, this is my friend Janice?" Or is it, "Janice, this is my mom and dad?" Propriety calls for presenting the younger person to the older or more esteemed person: "senator Smith, this is my mother and father."

The foregoing discussion is a bit pretentious, perhaps, but social ability is high on the list of social maturity. Can you identify other public school programs and activities that serve to promote your social demeanor? High ability in math, science, and reading commonly receives the credit for being what's important in school learning. Student tests on social and civil values are seldom or never administered. The lack of student discipline is a common complaint of schools today. We contend that the improvement of student social skills and civil behaviors should indeed be one of the public school's important purposes. "A school as a learning organization makes lessons learned—whether good or bad—available to all staff" (OCED 2016, 10).

NEVERTHELESS, THE CRITICISM OF PUBLIC EDUCATION REMAINS WITH US

Criticism relative to public education in America and lack of high-quality scholarship on the part of students are high on the list of criticism on the part of the citizenry. Determining valid and reliable data on the academic standing of students in the United States is difficult at best. Not that academic achievement of public school students is not widely reported, but the reliability and validity of the data, the selection and makeup of the students who were included in the achievement testing, how the tests were administered, and what student population(s) were included in the testing outcomes are not always clear. For example, is the makeup of eighth-grade students in the United States the same as eighth-grade students in all other countries?

In every research report that we examined for any particular student achievement results, some follow-up criticism of the research report or the organization that conducted the study commonly was brought forth by some other "authority" that commented on the "flaws" in the research methodology or the bias of the group that administered the study.

To illustrate further the point of research pronouncements and following criticism of the conclusions reached, we present the work of Berliner and Biddle (1996) titled *The Manufactured Crisis*. The authors contended that the attack on American schools in the early 1980s was largely an unwarranted and manufactured plot of right-wing school voucher advocates. A strong support of education is contended. In a following review of the Berliner and Biddle's *The Manufactured Crisis* book, Lawrence C. Stedman (1996) strongly criticized the book by stating that he was sympathetic to the authors' concerns, but as a scholar himself, who specializes in this kind of material, he found the analysis of Berliner and Biddle deeply flawed and misleading. He commented that the analysis mischaracterized the test score decline data, mishandled the international findings, and failed to acknowledge students' continuing low levels of academic achievement.

Nevertheless, it appears that the low levels of student achievement commonly reported in the literature are sealed in the minds of American citizens and a variety of reasons is set forth by the citizenry as to why this underachievement of American students is occurring. In chapter 3, we detail recommendations for meeting the challenge of low student achievement.

At the outset, the misconception that every eighth-grade student is to meet the same standard of achievement academically is flawed. It is similar to setting the height of three-and-a-half feet for all eighth-grade students to clear in the high jump by the end of the year. One group of students will clear the heights on their first try. A second group would likely clear that height by the end of eighth grade. A certain group of eighth-grade students will never be able to clear three-and-a-half feet at the end of the school year. Few persons would disagree with the fact that students differ, but education programs commonly require every student to meet the same levels of academic performance.

POST-CHAPTER QUIZ

Take just a few minutes to complete the following chapter quiz. The following ten multiple-choice questions serve as a review of important information that sets the stage for the following chapters.

Directions: Circle the best answer to each question that follows. Then check your response with the correct answers set forth at the end of the quiz.

1. One primary contention set forth in this chapter is that historically there has been
    a. little or no criticism of public school education across the fifty states.
    b. little or no support of public school education across the fifty states.
    c. much criticism of public school education but all such criticism has been proven unfounded by specific research findings.
    d. a specific equal and opposite response has been made to virtually every criticism directed toward public school education.
    e. sufficient available research on the quality of public school education to state that it is not failing in any sense of the word.

2. Which of the following factors are **not** viewed as an inhibitor to the success of public education in America?
    a. Inadequate financial support
    b. Inequities in program opportunities among the states
    c. Widening loss of local control of public education
    d. The percentage of high school graduates who continue their education by entering college
    e. Unsatisfactory student academic performance

3. Statistics relative to the financial support of public education have revealed that the ability to pay for public school education
    a. is virtually equal among the fifty states.
    b. differs as much as six to one, with the richest state's property value being six times that of the poorest state.
    c. differs only at the rate of two to one.
    d. is based on the amount of product sales since public school monies depend on this tax source.
    e. is determined by the state government differentials between sales income and purchasing costs.

4. Criticism of public school education has been
    a. an ongoing practice in educational history.
    b. a matter of poor school board policy decisions.

c. a political difference between the Republican and Democratic parties.
   d. due to the federal teachers' association attempts to control teachers' salaries.
   e. on an increase of 5 percent annually since the passing of the teacher tenure law in the 1940s.

5. Historically, public school education has been viewed as

   a. a federal responsibility.
   b. a state function.
   c. a local responsibility.
   d. a federal concern, a state responsibility, and a local function.
   e. None of the above.

6. Which entry below is commonly considered to be the **primary** responsibility of a local school board?

   a. Hiring of the teaching staff
   b. Public relations
   c. Hiring of the school superintendent
   d. School district governance policy development
   e. Professional negotiations with the school district's personnel
   f. None of the above.

7. The five U.S. states that were ranked highest in educational quality in one major research report were

   a. among those states with the lowest per-pupil support funding.
   b. among those states with the highest per-pupil support funding.
   c. considered to be in the medium of per-pupil support funding.
   d. states that did not include athletics or elementary school recess in their local school programs.
   e. states that had a special education tax on all goods sold within the state.

8. Virtually every report or study that centers on the quality of public education in America underscores the importance of

   a. establishing a mandatory system of student achievement accompanied by an in-grade retention system that demands the achievement of established grade standards for every subject and grade level in the school system.
   b. a change of school organization from the traditional K–12 school organization to an open-classroom system whereby the students themselves choose what they need to learn that day or that term in an open-classroom setting.
   c. federal support and control of public school curriculum offerings and the instructional methods to accompany them.

d. using ability level separation of students especially in the subject areas of reading, math, and science.
e. None of the above.
f. All of the above.

9. When all is said and done, it is clear that public education in America
   a. is failing.
   b. is a success.
   c. has identifiable factors that inhibit high-quality education for all students everywhere.
   d. has identifiable factors that promote quality education for all students everywhere.
   e. None of the above.
   f. All of the above.

10. The contents in this chapter tend to suggest that
    a. public school education in the United States is failing.
    b. public school education in the United States is succeeding.
    c. public education in the United States can be "saved" only if local school districts would give priority to professional development programs for all professional staff.
    d. traditional public education in the United States would be privatized and become competitive among the various "business parties" similar to competitive parties in business and industry.
    e. None of the above.
    f. All of the above.

TRUE OR FALSE

1. Research studies and collected evidence make it clear that public school education is failing. T___, or F___?
2. Among the many critical factors facing public school education, the factor of financial support is seldom named among the top ten problems and issues. T___, or F___?
3. Those individuals in education with some experience commonly name the lack of research as a cause of educational failure. T___, or F___?
4. Unfortunately, no one has ever set forth a recommendation for changes in compensating school personnel that would theoretically improve the hiring and retention of teachers. T___, or F___?
5. Research evidence has made it clear that education inequities among the states can be remedied by the federal government's intervention into public school education. T___, or F___?

6. The statistics relative to the fifty states have shown that the ability to support education financially differs on a ratio of six to one. T___, or F___?
7. Successful school programs set forth academic standards that every child must meet before moving ahead. T___, or F___?
8. Basic research accomplished in education is one factor that underscores the current success of public school operations. T___, or F___?
9. Interestingly enough, no authority or educational group has ever set forth specific alternatives for compensating teachers in public schools. T___, or F___?
10. Public education in America is viewed as a state responsibility. T___, or F___?

DISCUSSION OF THE POST-CHAPTER QUIZ

We introduced a post-chapter quiz in this chapter to underscore its purpose of examining the wide division of views relative to the current effectiveness of public education in America and examining the major reasons why educational reforms seldom result in long-term improvements or wide public acceptance of implemented reform interventions.

Question #1

In question #1, the reader was asked to complete the question: One primary contention is that historically there has been which one of the five possible responses? The best response to the question is "d": "a specific and equal response has been made to virtually every criticism directed toward public education." There are multiple examples of this troublesome controversy. For example, McSpadden's article "Public Schools Aren't Failing" (2015) was countered by DeSilver's article "U.S. Students' Academic Achievement Still Lags That of Their Peers in Many Other Countries" (2017).

The question for our consideration centers on what professional leadership and program promotions are to be pursued in depth. Even the matter of educational support for public education has its pro and con audiences. In many instances, the yes or no answer is vested in an educational matter that is definitely political in nature. The promotion of charter schools, local school control, school curricular offerings, and school funding are prime examples of political education decision matters.

Question #2

The correct response to question #2 is "d," "the percentage of high school graduates who continue their education by entering college." In the year

2009, an all-time high of 70.1 percent of the high school graduates were enrolled in college. In a later 2013 report, this percentage had dropped to 65.9 percent but raised again to 69.7 percent in 2016. In the more recent years between 2011 and 2016, the percentage of enrolled high school graduates increased only 1.4 percent. The highest enrollment of recent high school graduates was in 2009, with an enrollment figure of 70.1 percent. The high school graduation figure has tended to retain its relative high percentage of college enrollees in spite of increases in high school student dropout rates, governmental emphasis on vocational/technical education in the 1960s, and the calls for military service on the part of male and female graduates during the various military "conflicts" over the years.

Some persons would argue that college entrance data on the part of high school graduates are an inhibiting factor as opposed to a success factor of public education. Many other factors serve to influence such decisions, including job opportunities, ability to pay higher college tuition fees, academic standing, and vocational/technical program interests.

Question #3

The answer to question #3 is "b," whereby the richest states' ability to pay is six times that of other poorest states. Since local taxes on property values serve specifically for education support, the inequities of funding are major concerns for giving each child in the United States a fair and equal opportunity for a quality education. Various financial support methods have been designed by the several states. Nevertheless, major differences in property values make equalizing financial support per child a difficult situation. Providing a required minimum education support might well be relatively easy to do for some school districts but may also place a hardship on districts with limited property values. This issue is discussed additionally in a later chapter.

Question #4

Criticism of public school education has been "a," "an ongoing practice in education history." Who should be educated? How education should be financially supported? What should be emphasized in the public school curriculum? Should student in-grade retention be discontinued or increased? Should standardized testing of student academic performance be increased and used as a basis for determining a teacher's salary? Should recess at the elementary school level be discontinued? Who or what body should be solely responsible for determining the curricular program of a public school? Why does the state have so many separate school districts that need separate school boards, more principals, and more school facilities? Does class size really make a difference in student achievement? What specific program interventions would actually serve to end the criticism of education in the United States? Will such a solution ever be found?

Question #5

Historically, public school education has been viewed as, "d," "a federal concern, a state responsibility, and a local function." It has been noted that the U.S. Constitution makes no mention of education but the Tenth Amendment leaves those matters not specifically mentioned in the document to the states and their people. Thus, such matters as vocational/technical education, physical education, students with special needs, improved math/science instruction, and many others have been high on the list of federal concerns. Educational interventions by the federal government, state government, and other parties have lessened the local control of education. The development of policy manuals for local school districts by the National Association of School Boards is a prime example. Retaining local control of education, state mandates, and federal interventions have been major debates on educational matters historically.

Question #6

"Which entry below is considered to be the primary responsibility of the local school board?" The answer is "f," "none of the above." We do understand that many knowledgeable individuals would have circled entry "c," "the hiring of the school superintendent," or perhaps entry "d," "public relations." However, as stated by Norton, "The development of school district policies is the most important responsibility of school boards nationally . . . Effective policy development is the crux of successful school operation" (2017, vii). Administrative procedures, local school control, professional development program activities, and operational success are inextricably tied to the effective policies that focus on the goals and objectives, which the school district is destined to achieve.

Question #7

The five states that were ranked highest in education quality in one major research report were "among those states with the highest per-pupil support funding," answer "b." For example, in one study of education quality, the state of Massachusetts was ranked number one. That state was also among those states with the highest per-pupil financial support. Although this relationship does not ring perfect for all states, the fact that per-pupil spending is related to education quality is notable in reliable study reports.

Question #8

Virtually, every report or study that centers on the quality of education in America underscores the matter of "e," "none of the above." Although each of the five entries set forth as possible answers has been proposed in some form by somebody over time, no research report or *long-term* school program has featured any of these five outcomes (e.g., mandatory system of student achievement accompanied by an in-grade retention system, change from K–12 school organization to an open-classroom system, federal support and control of education, separation of students by ability level). We do emphasize long-term programs, since similar organizational arrangements have been implemented for brief time periods historically.

Question #9

When all is said and done, it is clear that public school education in America "has identifiable factors that inhibit quality education for all students everywhere," answer "c," and "has identifiable factors that promote quality education for all students everywhere," answer "d." Both "c" and "d" responses appear to be in order. The question is vested in what approach is to be taken for reaching the objective of making education in America the best of all worlds. Is it best to give primary attention to improving and/or reimagining the factors that are inhibiting quality education or is it best to focus on those factors that are fostering quality education in public education? The oversimplification of an answer to these questions is to focus on both. The following chapters of the book center on both approaches. However, reimagining education rather than additional attention to more reforms is given emphasis in future chapters.

Question #10

The contents of this chapter tend to suggest that "e," "none of the above," response is completely correct. That is, no conclusions can be reached to set forth the result that public education is indeed failing or succeeding. Characteristics of failure were identified, and the same thing can be said for education's success. Our approach to this result is that researched innovations must be taken to keep improving and extending those factors that are having successful educational results, and revolutionary concepts must be implemented to extinguish those factors that are failing and establish revolutionary changes in educational practice.

Answers to the True or False Questions

#1 is False, #2 is False, #3 is False, #4 is False, #5 is False, #6 is True, #7 is False, #8 is False, #9 is False, and #10 is True. Various studies have set forth a variety of reasons why public schools are failing. Thus, statement #1 is false. The fact is that there is a wide difference of opinion as to whether public schools are failing or doing well. In regard to statement #2, financial support for education rises near or at the top of reasons why public schools are failing. Chapter 3 makes it clear that statement #3 is false. Research is seldom mentioned within education discussions for supporting or criticizing public school outcomes. Chapter 3 discusses various needed changes in public school programming and changes in the way teachers are compensated is one of them. Thus, statement #4 is false. No such research has been set forth regarding the intervention of the federal government for "saving" public schools in America; statement #5 is false. Statement #6 is true; the ability to support education differs considerably among the fifty states. The ratio of 6 to 1 represents the extent to which financial support for education differs from highest to lowest ability. Statement #7 is false. Students differ and thus one set standard sets forth an inequitable expectation for student achievement results. There has been no such research on educational standards as suggested in statement #8; thus #8 is false. It is true that Klein (2011) and others have recommended major changes in the way public school teachers are compensated. Thus, statement #9 is false.

THOUGHTS ON WHAT IS RIGHT WITH PUBLIC EDUCATION

A general statement by Kowal and Thomas (2002) serves to sum up what commonly is viewed by the citizenry as to what is right with public education.

American tradition of public education began with Jefferson's ideal of an aristocracy based on talent and not on inherited wealth and privilege. Ever since its inception, the grand tradition of public education has undergone significant changes. It has been a crucial part of the immigrant experience, allowing the children of first-generation Americans to achieve a level of success that would not have been possible in their native countries. Indeed, education has produced a level of social mobility that is unmatched in most countries. It is public education that helps create a shared culture that is essential in any democracy. Public education also nurtures the financial health of any society.

Key Chapter Ideas and Recommendations

- Reports and opinions regarding the quality of public schools differ widely. When one criticism of education is set forth that education is failing, another opinion comes forth claiming that public school education is better than ever before. The major criticisms of public school education center on the lack of financial support, inequities in the quality of education programs within the states and school districts, the extension of state and federal agencies into the control of local education programs, the incompetency of both teacher and administrative personnel, and poor student academic achievement.

- Empirical evidence makes it quite clear that American citizenry not only differs on whether the public schools are failing or not but they also differ widely on the purposes of public school education. One most frequently stated purpose is that of the need for an educated citizenry sustaining a democratic form of government. Others tend to be of the opinion that public school education should focus on resolving the many social issues being encountered in the nation that tend to find their way into the public schools of America as well. It is clear that both of these purposes need to be reimagined and resolved.

- The highest ranking of states relative to quality education is closely correlated with the highest per-pupil spending; that is, the highest-ranking states for quality also spend most on per-pupil education support.

- The ability to pay for education among the states differs from 6 to 1. That is, the state with the highest property value has six times the property value of the lowest state's property value.

- The lack of policy development on the part of local school boards has resulted in a lessening of their local control of the education program. The responsibility for developing policy at the local school level has been turned over to state school board associations in an increasing number of cases. It is recommended that this practice be stopped. The primary responsibility of school boards should be the development of guiding school policy. School board associations have many other things to do. Just assisting local school districts in establishing an effective codification system for policy manuals is one such service.

- The increasing inability of school districts to recruit and retain high-quality teachers and administrative personnel is among education's leading problems. Quality instruction and high-level student learning will never take place without the presence of high-quality education personnel.

- Administrative mismanagement within public schools looms as a major inhibitor of quality education. Mismanagement has major implications for education financial support, professional education preparation programs, and competency performance on the job.

- The lack of major research units within the local school districts and state education offices looms as a primary cause of public school failure. The failure to establish high-quality research programs within local school districts and state departments of education is a critical error on the part of educational services within the fifty states. In professions such as medicine and other successful business and industrial practices, research is the foundation of progress and success. If a cure for cancer or Alzheimer's disease was found in medical research, practicing professionals around the world would have the results of the research in place as a first priority. In education, when viable results of research are found in relation to student retention, class size, student learning styles, and other practices, educators tend to continue doing what they have been doing for many years.

- The hiring of teacher personnel who have not completed a training program is more serious perhaps than is realized by the general public. No one would knowingly go to a physician, lawyer, or other professional service provider who had not completed satisfactorily the preparation requirements for licensing. Yet, this practice in education has been increasing and certain testing results are reflecting its outcome.

- Major success factors in public school education include the wide range of academic opportunities that students have available for learning, the inclusiveness of public schools and openness for children of all abilities and interests, the improvement of teacher preparation programs over the years, the high percentage of high school graduates who enroll in college, the program guidance given to students relative to the culture of the American society, the importance of education to maintain a democratic form of national governance, and supporting the American concept of a free enterprise system, which can be credited in large part to the work of America's public education provisions.

Yet, criticism of America's public school system remains. The following chapters of the book center on what it will take to reimagine education in our country. Educational reform is not the term that we have in mind. Rather, revolutionary reimagining of ways for making public education the best of all worlds will serve the discussions provided in the chapters that follow.

Discussion Questions

1. Assume that you are a member of a debate team that is debating the following resolution: "Resolved: Public Education Is Failing." Take sides as a member of the "pros" or the "cons" debate team and write out your two-minute opening statement for your team.

2. Put on your reimagination hat and give thought to the preparation of teachers as you understand it today. If you are or have been a teacher, what changes would you recommend in the preparation program in which you engaged? If not a teacher, rely on what you know and have observed relative to teaching performance. How might you add to or change the preparation programs for teachers or what provisions in teacher preparation do you believe are the most significant? Can you come up with a revolutionary preparation program model?

3. This chapter set forth the statement that the quality of an education system cannot exceed the quality of teachers. What does this concept suggest for needed changes in public education practices and financial support?

4. Take a moment to review the success factors for education set forth in this chapter. What additional success factor(s) might you add to that listing? Set forth a brief defense of your response.

5. At a parent–teacher meeting at your school, the matter of increasing student fees for certain subjects, sport's participation, and related program activities came to the floor. One parent commented that she believed that the American way was that each student was assured the right to a free and equal education. What might be your response to the parent's belief?

Case Study
Just a Matter of Working Harder or Is It?

Principal Woolhether was meeting with the school faculty to give them the unfortunate news that their school had just received a rating of "C" as being underperforming.

"We need to act and act now," said Principal Woolhether, "I am required to respond to this situation within two months with details of what we plan to do to reverse this failing trend. Of course, the test results focus on math, science and reading scores, so this has to be our major focus."

"What changes are to be made in our program activities and instructional strategies?" asked Mr. Evans. "What about the instructional resources that we need and the student apathy that all of us are facing? What about the new textbooks that have been on order for at least two years?"

"I am concerned about the present mandate that sets forth the instructional methods for the teaching of reading," inserted Miss Ortez. "It's like someone is looking over my shoulder and telling me how to teach. I took two courses on reading for my Bachelor's degree and believe that I know something about the subject of reading."

"Yeah," responded Coach Adams, who also taught science. "Do we get new kids?"

After the laughter died down, Principal Woolhether cautioned the faculty about making excuses and went on to say, "We need to change and the sooner the better. Just setting forth excuses will not suffice. Now let's all get to work!"

Case Study Discussion Questions

1. What seems to be missing from Principal Woolhether's closing remarks of "Now let's get back to work!"
2. How might the information on organizational development (OD) set forth in the chapter be most helpful in the study case? Although the case calls for a response on the matter within two months, what information might be sent back as a first response in order for an effective OD procedure to be planned, implemented, evaluated, and assessed?

REFERENCES

Abeler, J., and Jaeger, S. (2015). "Complex Tax Incentives." *American Economic Policy* 7 (3): 1–28.

Barber, M. and Mourshed M. (2007). "How the World's Best-Performing School Systems Come Out on Top." Report. McKinsey & Company website. https://www.mckinsey.com/industries/social-sector/our-insights/how-the-worlds-best-performing-school-systems-come-out-on-top.

Berliner, D. C., and Biddle, B. J. (1996). *The Manufactured Crisis: Myths, Fraud, and the Attack on America's Public Schools*. New York: Basic Books.

Bernardo, R. (2018). "2018's Most and Least Education States in America." *WalletHub*, January 23. https://wallethub.com/edu/most-educated-states/31075/.

Biddle, B. J., and Berliner, D. C. (2002). "A Research Synthesis / Unequal School Funding in the United States." *Beyond Instructional Leadership* 59 (8): 48–59. http://www.ascd.org/publications/educational-leadership/may02/vol59/num08/Unequal-School-Funding-in-the-United-States.aspx.

Cano, R. (2018a). "State Will Take Over Murphy School District." *Arizona Republic*, June 26, 1A.

Cano, R. (2018b). "Thousands of Teachers Lack Complete Formal Training." *Arizona Republic* (azcentral.com), August 23. https://www.azcentral.com/story/news/local/arizona-education/2018/08/22/arizona-teacher-shortage-thousands-public-schools-untrained/1043860002/.

Chen, G. (2018). "Public School vs. Private School." *Public School Review* (blog), November 1. https://www.publicschoolreview.com/blog/public-school-vs-private-school.

Chuck, E. (2015). "Just Over Half of All College Students Actually Graduate, Report Finds." *NBC News*, November 18. https://www.nbcnews.com/feature/freshman-year/just-over-half-all-college-students-actually-graduate-report-finds-n465606.

Conant, J. B. (1959). *The American High School Today: A First Report to Interested Citizens*. Carnegie Series in American Education. New York: McGraw-Hill.

DeSilver, D. (2017). "U.S. Students' Academic Achievement Still Lags that of Their Peers in Many Other Countries." *Pew Research Center*, February 15. http://www.pewresearch.org/fact-tank/2017/02/15/u-s-students-internationally-math-science/.

Fedewa, L. J. (2014). "American Schools are Failing!" *The Washington Post*, June 1. https://www.washingtontimes.com/news/2014/jun/1/fedewa-american-schools-are-failing/.

The Gates Foundation (2017). *What We Do: K–12 Education Strategy Overview*. gatesfoundation.org. https://www.gatesfoundation.org/What-We-Do/US-Program/K-12-Education.

Gupta, A. (2008). "What Is Organizational Development?" *Practical Management*. Practical Management Institute, Phoenix, AZ: Author.

Klein, J. (2011). "The Failure of Americna Schools." *The Atlantic*, June 11. https://www.theatlantic.com/magazine/archive/2011/06/the-failure-of-american-schools/308497/.

Kowal J. and Thomas T. M. (2002). "What's Right with Public Education: Fastback." *ERIC*. ERIC Number: EAD478534.

McSpadden, K. (2015). "Public Schools Aren't Failing." *The Charlotte Observer*, January 30. https://www.charlotteobserver.com/opinion/op-ed/article9499466.html.

Norton, M. S. (2017). *A Guide for Educational Policy Governance: Effective Leadership for Policy Development.* Lanham, MD: Rowman & Littlefield.

Norton, M. S. (2018). *Dealing with Change: The Effects of Organizational Development on Contemporary Practices.* Lanham, MD: Rowman & Littlefield.

Norton, M. S., Kelly, L. K., and Battle, A. R. (2012). *The Principal as Student Advocate: A Guide for Doing What's Best for All Students.* Larchmont, NY: Eye On Education.

OECD (2012). "Investing in Equity Pays Off." In *Equity in Education: Supporting Disadvantaged Students and Schools*, 13–45. Paris: OECD Publishing. https://doi.org/10.1787/9789264130852-3-en.

OECD (2016). *What Makes a School a Learning Organization?: A Guide for Policy Makers, School Leaders, and Teachers.* Paris: OECD Publishing.

Rampell, C. (2014). "Actually, Public Education Is Getting Better, Not Worse." *The Washington Post*, September 19. https://www.washingtonpost.com/opinions/catherine-rampell-actually-public-education-is-getting-better-not-worse/2014/09/18/7c23b020-3f6a-11e4-9587-5dafd96295f0_story.html?utm_term=.99fe1ec85ee7.

Rhee, M. A. (2011). "Merit Plan" (op-ed). *Wall Street Journal*, January 1.

Room 241 (2018). "Public Education Costs per Pupil by State Rankings" (blog post), April 6. https://education.cu-portland.edu/blog/classroom-resources/public-education-costs-per-pupil-by-state-rankings/.

Sager. J. (2013). "Why American Public Schools are Failing." *The Progressive Cynic (blog)*, May 6. https://theprogressivecynic.com/2013/05/06/why-american-public-schools-are-failing/.

Schneider, J. (2016). "America's Not-So-Broken Education System: Do U.S. Schools Really Need to be Disrupted?" *The Atlantic*, June 22. https://www.theatlantic.com/education/archive/2016/06/everything-in-american-education-is-broken/488189/.

Stedman, L. C. (1996). "The Achievement Crisis is Real: A Review of *The Manufactured Crisis.*" *Education Policy Analysis Archives* 4 (1). http://dx.doi.org/10.14507/epaa.v4n1.1996.

Chapter 2

Reimagining the Failing Factors of Public School Education

Primary chapter goal: To enhance the understanding of the financial issues facing education and the personnel issues that must be resolved before quality can be assured.

THERE IS NOTHING IMPOSSIBLE, OR IS THERE?

Chapter 1 discussed the problems of insufficient financial support for public schools and the inequities therein. Although the topic of funding education in America has been included in a myriad of legislative actions, written articles, and reports, such declarations are commonly vested in statements that we simply need more money or we need to reorganize school districts or we must cut the overlapping of administrative functions or we must clear up the mismanagement of schools or we must do something else. It isn't that legislators have not tried various "solutions" such as taxing the rich to pay for the needy, but such actions simply have not worked.

At the time of this writing, leaders of Invest in Education in Arizona had collected 270,000 signatures, twice the 150,642 valid signatures the campaign needed for the measure to qualify for the November ballot. The ballot would bring in $690 million in funding for public schools by nearly doubling the income tax rate on Arizona's highest earners. Ricardo Cano (2018a) of the *Arizona Republic* reported that the measure would raise income tax rates by 3.46 percentage points on individuals who earn more than $250,000 and households that earn more than $500,000, by 4.46 percentage points on individuals who earn more than $500,000 and households that earn more than $1 million. This strategy has been referred to as the "Robinhood concept" in that it is viewed as robbing the rich to give to the poor.

The foregoing strategy for funding education raises questions in the minds of many persons. One letter to the editor of the *Arizona Republic* asked the following question with tongue in cheek, "Shouldn't we punish those who've dared to succeed?" The writer asks the question of: "How dare some Arizona citizens start at the bottom, get an education, work their way up the ladder and become successful? Here in Arizona shouldn't we punish those who dare to succeed?" It doesn't seem to matter how much these people already pay in state and federal taxes, are still paying in student loans, and already are contributing to the school-community, they have more than others and education needs it.

It is relatively easy to find instances whereby large amounts of money are available for things that would be viewed by thinking persons as being far less important than the education of our citizenry. Today, a professional teacher with five years of experience might, on the average, be earning $56,000 a year. In the *Arizona Republic* on July 4, 2018, it was reported that a star guard for a professional basketball team will be earning $31,600,000 a year. Comparing apples and oranges, of course, but something is wrong here with America's priorities.

How do many teachers make ends meet? According to Will (2018), 20 percent of them hold down a second job. The statistics of the National Center for Education Labor state that the average teacher's salary is $38,617 and that figure lags the overall starting wage of $50,359 for graduates with a bachelor's degree in all fields. None of the teachers who hold second jobs get rich. As noted by Will, teachers who have second jobs earn an average annual salary of $5,100. Part of these earnings, $479, is commonly paid by teachers themselves for necessary school supplies. In any case, it is reasonable to conclude that having outside of school work can result in additional stress and less attention given to their primary responsibilities as a classroom teacher.

The matter of teachers having to pay for their own classroom supplies, on the cover, seems to be somewhat of a nonconsequential concern. After all, the teaching profession isn't the only profession where the "worker" has to supply the tools to do the job. Yet, teachers say that the monies that they do receive for such purpose are not enough and parents are becoming distraught by the constant requests from the teacher to pay more each year for school supplies in order to cover the gap (Castle and Juarez 2018).

In addition, many of the supplies are not only for teachers but also for students whose parents cannot afford to do so. This is education in America, the best of all worlds?

Once again, we are reminded of the paramount problem of teacher turnover. Consider the situation whereby a school district hires fifty new teachers. After only one year, an estimated 20 percent to 30 percent of this group of teachers leave the profession. An effective organization cannot withstand such employee instability. The upfront costs of recruiting and hiring new personnel, orienting new personnel to the school and school district's purposes and procedures, in-service program expenses, and other development activities are virtually lost; a new cycle of recruiting and hiring must begin once again.

If citizens were asked to rank the importance of the following five activities for America's future, one would guess that an effective education program for the citizenry, maintenance of a strong military force, an effective program of health care, maintenance of a strong economic program, and an effective security system of law and order would result in placing education of the citizenry on or near the top of the list. Unfortunately, having the world's best professional football or basketball team might rank first in several states.

San Antonio Independent School District v. Rodriguez

Alana Samuels (2016) speaks of the most aggressive attempts to improve the disparities among states and school districts. In this case, a father, Demetrio Rodriguez, sued the state of Texas for what, he determined, was not justified under the U.S. Constitution's equal protection clause. That is, every child in every school district was guaranteed an equal opportunity to education. In the Rodriguez case, the court ruled to the contrary stating that the Constitution included no right to equal funding for education. Law suits on educational funding have been rampant in virtually every state since the 1973 court ruling in the Rodriguez case.

The "No Solution" Responses

First, we need no additional publications that inform us that public school funding within and among the states is unequal. Article after article has been written on inequity and its arguments regarding how this effects student performance. A prime example is an article by Biddle and Berliner (2002) titled "A Research Synthesis/Unequal School Funding in the United States." After writing many pages on what is already known about funding inequities within the states and using forty references to support what the profession already knows, the authors set forth four nonsolution paragraphs such as, "Become familiar with the facts and issues associated with equity and funding in U.S. schools, the unsupportable claims about funding effects sometimes made by those who oppose equitable funding, and the research findings that contradict those claims" (15).

A Revolutionary Move toward a Solution: Thinking Outside the Proverbial Box

Most citizens are aware that the Constitution of the United States does not mention the word "education" among its contents. The Constitution was ratified 230 years ago in 1788. The nation has utilized the wording of the Preamble to the U.S. Constitution for authorizing the states to act on those matters not directly set forth in the Constitution. Yet, the intervention of the federal government in public education over the years has increased substantially. Federal officials use the general welfare statements set forth in the Preamble to the U.S. Constitution and in the Taxing and Spending Clause for their "authority" to act on public school issues.

So, if such action on the part of the federal government is possible and apparently legal, why can't it act on the major issue of equity in public education support? The welfare statement has been debated in an ongoing fashion within the government and in the courts. The growth of public education and its corresponding needs are much different today than when the U.S. Constitution was being drafted. If adopted today, how might the important matter of public education be treated?

Over the years, our national presidents have expressed the paramount importance of an effective public school program as being essential to the nation's democratic republic, sustaining the American system of a free business enterprise, and as the best thing that can be done to give each and every individual an equal chance and fair start in the race life. Today, it is difficult not to find the federal government involved in public school education. Yet, the federal government is supporting education monetarily to only 10 percent compared to the approximate support of a state's 45 percent and the local school district support of 45 percent.

There are twenty-seven amendments to the U.S. Constitution with the last amendment being introduced as early as 1789 but not officially ratified until 1992, more than 200 years later. The Twenty-Seventh Amendment prohibits any law that increases or decreases the salary of members of Congress from taking effect until the starting of the next set of terms for representatives.

Is a Call for a Twenty-Eighth Amendment for Public Schools a Step toward Education Becoming the Best of All Worlds?

The following is a thought outside the proverbial box. Is the present stalemate for public education support a possible call for a new Twenty-Eighth Amendment to the U.S. Constitution? That is, might public education in America become a federal *responsibility*, a state *concern*, and a local function?

Although financial support would become the primary responsibility of the federal government, both the states and local school districts could supplement financial support as well. But, wait, wouldn't such a major change permit the federal government to control public school education? Yes, to a greater extent than now, but the Twenty-Eighth Amendment could be written to clarify educational purposes of assuring equity for students within all of the fifty states with the fifty states and local communities serving the important role of determining the procedures as to how best these purposes are met.

That Isn't Going to Happen. That's Absurd. That Would Destroy Local Control

Kumar (2014) quoted Miguel de Cervantes as saying, "In order to attain the impossible, one must attempt to be absurd." And as emphasized by Kumar, "Look at the Wright brothers for example . . . The brothers were not as prepared and not as well funded with elaborate teams and equipment as their competitors. They could have said, 'This is absurd and impossible.' Instead they made it happen" (4). Greg Satell (2015) makes an important point in his article, "How the Impossible Becomes Possible." He notes, "Things like a quantum internet or self-driving cars that seemed like pipe dreams a decade ago are now realities. In a decade or two, we'll all be using them" (4). A trip to the moon, an impossibility, became possible in 1969. Then, what about the possibility of a Twenty-Eighth Amendment on national education?

Thinking Far Outside the Proverbial Box

The Twenty-Eighth Amendment to the U.S. Constitution: As It Might Be Proposed

A new Twenty-Eighth Amendment would view public education in the United States as a major responsibility of the federal government and as such would serve to set forth the purposes of public education and assure equity and fairness for all children and youth. State and local agencies are granted the authority to establish administrative regulations for implementing educational programs that carry out the purposes established by the federal government. That is, decisions on how to meet the goals and standards, such as the choice of teaching techniques and the purchase of supplies, are best left to schools as long as effective monitoring and assessment program requirements are in place. Equity and inclusiveness of education are primary conditions of responsibility in establishing effective educational programs in the various states.

Does it make any sense that presently a child has virtually no choice as to where he or she lives and goes to school? If the child is born and raised in New Mexico, Mississippi, Arizona, or one of the other states where education quality is ranked as being low and is supported financially at a lower level, there is a good possibility that the child will not continue to work and live in that state for life. In fact, due to mobility in today's world, the individual might live and work in several different states. We contend that the fair and equitable answer is that the child should receive a quality education regardless of the circumstances that placed the individual in one state or another at the outset of life. And once again, even if equity were to be possible within one state, inequity among the fifty states would remain inevitable. The contention is that equity is a good possibility with national oversight.

Approving a new special education tax does place an additional "burden" on tax payers. Such an act does not repeal the high property taxes already paid on business sales, property owners, renters, and those who own homes. A question of importance is to ask just why states are not able to support education financially in the first place. Among the primary reasons is the fact that governance agencies have gone overboard in their efforts to attract businesses and, in doing so, have excused them from paying taxes for many years. Of course, someone benefits by excusing tax payments of large new businesses, but the evidence has shown that it has not been education.

But Wouldn't a Twenty-Eighth Amendment on Education Lead to a National Curriculum?

The answer to the title question above is inevitably "yes." But what does such a change really mean? A national curriculum is commonly viewed as a set of subjects and standards used by K–12 schools for students to learn specific information. It covers what subjects are taught and the standards that students should reach in each subject. Sounds a lot like the common core that schools throughout the states have complained about for several years. Nevertheless, there are five specific statements that serve to describe a national school curriculum. It most likely would appear to the reader that we are proposing a national curriculum for America's schools. In fact, this is not the case. The focus of this chapter is to address the problem of inequity whereby major program innovations are likely to be required to meet the goal of an equitable education for every student in every state.

What are the major components of a national curriculum? The following conditions are directly related to a national curriculum:

1. Every state-funded school must offer a curriculum that is balanced and broadly based. Such a curriculum promotes the spiritual, moral, cultural,

mental, and physical development of pupils at the school and prepares pupils at the school for the opportunities, responsibilities, and experiences of later life. (Can you accept this first entry?)

2. The curriculum comprises all learning and other experiences that each school plans for its pupils. The national curriculum forms one part of the school curriculum. (Each school is doing the program planning. Can you accept this second entry?)

3. Maintained schools are legally required to follow the statutory national curriculum that sets out in programs of study, on the basis of key stages, content for these subjects that should be taught to all pupils. (That is, entry #1 must be followed as appropriate for the stages of student development.)

4. All schools should make provision for personal, social, health, and economic curriculum, drawing on good practice. Schools are also free to include other subjects or topics of their choice in planning and designing their own programs of education.

It is noted that entry #4 is worth additional consideration. It places a great deal of responsibility and choice on the part of each local school. Local control is given serious consideration and primary opportunities to lead at the local school level.

Note that the foregoing curriculum components are based on factual national school curriculum requirements in England (gov.uk 2013). Once again, such requirements are noted for one purpose, the reader's information. It should be noted that the national curriculum in England includes a daily act of collective worship and must teach religious education to pupils. This requirement is purposely omitted here due to America's belief in the separation of church and state. Keep in mind that quality and equity in educational opportunities for students are the overriding considerations in this discussion.

Other Educational Financial Support Interventions

The problems of educational funding remain unresolved. Trying to increase funding by way of car washes and course subject fees falls far short of education needs. The concept of building foundations to fund significant causes, while being reported as successful in some school districts (New 2012), is sporadic and falls short of serving toward the goal of having education in America the best of all worlds. Taking chances with fund-raising is not the savior for quality and equity education throughout the nation. As reported by Bob New (2012), "Out of Pennsylvania's 500 school districts, there are 215 education foundations, many of these just recently established. Few have been able to effectively attract the significant donor funding required to offset the loss of government funding so far" (n.p.).

A recommendation was made by the writer, New, for school districts to contact The Foundation for Enhancing Communities located in Harrisburg, Pennsylvania, that reportedly was among those active foundations for educational purposes. In doing so, a report was found that took place on September 3, 2015, whereby the foundation had awarded $5,320 to the Lion Foundation for benches and a hitting board for the Camp Hill Borough Siebert Park tennis courts. It appears obvious that while foundations might provide some financial support for schools, relying on them to solve the inequity problems is not going to happen.

Imagine What Might Result If Educational Funding Were to Support Education Success

As a case in point, imagine that a funding program for education reached the ability to compete for personnel talents commensurate with lawyers, business executives, primary physicians, engineers, dentists, and other major professions. Each of the aforementioned professions has their importance in our society, but only education is given the primary importance of serving to maintain a democratic governance, the free enterprise system so crucial in the improvement of America's standards of living, and as stated by President Lincoln, the one thing that can give each citizen a free start and fair chance in the race of life.

Kowai and Thomas (2002) spoke of what is right with public education. In doing so, they underscored the fact that public education is the only place where children have the opportunity to learn under the positive conditions of caring teachers. In addition, public education's role in sharing a shared culture is of paramount importance for sustaining a democracy. They, too, underscore the point of education's importance in creating the financial health of any society that serves for the betterment of every citizen and their standard of living.

Important Differences of Funding between the United States and Other Countries

Some ideas of resolving education inequalities are provided in information set forth by Biddle and Berliner (2002). These writers note that the United States is the only nation that supports educational funding on the sole basis of local wealth. Other countries, such as the Netherlands, for example, base funding on student enrollment, but also for every guilder allocated to a middle-class child, additional guilders are allocated for every lower-class child and for a minority child, which the authors claim is just the opposite of what commonly is done in the United States where lower-class and minority children receive less than middle-class white children. One guilder (NLG) is equal to about 49 cents in U.S. currency.

Funding programs in some districts throughout the United States have attempted to change procedures; some have improved inequality problems, and others have been challenged and ruled unconstitutional by the courts. The foregoing information was set forth in 2002, sixteen years ago. Nevertheless, it gives "food for thought" for states that have not examined and altered their funding programs if inequities are still present in their support programs.

States Have Tried to Gain Equity among School Districts

Available literature on the subject makes it clear that many states have given much attention to the matter of equity for their public school districts. After the Vermont Supreme Court ruling that the state's education funding was unconstitutional, in 1997 the state passed Act 60 that was to assure that the towns spent the same amount of revenue per pupil (Samuels 2016). Other states such as New Jersey and California have had their state funding systems ruled unconstitutional. Efforts to rectify the unconstitutional rulings commonly have left the states without the resources to pay for education and the deficiencies of support leave the public schools in a downward spiral.

High-Quality Personnel: The *Sine Quo Non* for Education Being the Best of All Worlds

"America has yet to face seriously the facts of teacher supply, teacher recruitment, quality teachers, teacher compensation, and teacher retention" (Norton 2017, 51). The goal of making education the best of all worlds will not be achieved unless education has the highest quality of teachers and administrative personnel. This achievement will never happen unless the American citizenry does not only want the best education but also gives education the kind of financial support that attracts and retains the best personnel in the world.

Educational improvements are not just about needed funds for today's school personnel. As former president Richard Nixon contended, just pouring more money into education will not improve it. However, having the monetary funds to attract, prepare, recruit, hire, and retain high-quality personnel is the goal to be achieved. There are no intentions here of downgrading those high-performing teachers presently on the job; but putting new money into failing schools and expecting miracles is a flawed concept.

Later, in this chapter, the major changes needed in promoting education as a life profession for talented personnel are discussed. Such promotion does not begin at the time the individual enters college but long before as the student has opportunity to learn the paramount importance of education from the standpoint of country, self-fulfillment, community life, and personal values. In the best of all worlds, educators are valued in the same sense that other highly respected personnel such as physicians, professors, CEOs, government leaders, and other professionals are revered. Educators should be revered for who they are and what they do.

Professions That Are Part of the School Curriculum

It is interesting to consider the curriculum in our public schools in relation to the major professions in America. For example, most school programs include the following course work: each course has implications for career professions. It is not the contention to complain on these careers implications; rather, it is to underscore the need for such information to be considered relative to the positive aspects of a career in the educational profession.

A recent article in a local newspaper was titled "High School Volunteers Learning Medical Field." Since the beginning of the program in 2006, it has involved more than 1,360 teens who were learning more about hospitals and health care (USA Today Network 2018, Z10). Student participants have the opportunity to work on medical research and creative projects, escort patients, perform administrative duties, work alongside staff who mentor them, and more. The summer volunteer program offers in-depth learning and leadership opportunity for teens interested in the healthcare industry. As stated by the supervisor of the program, "We want to encourage them to learn about the variety of careers available in the medical field" (Z10).

Another medical program for high school students is reported by Yozwiak (2018). Forty-five student scholars spend eight weeks in TGen's laboratories receiving one-on-one mentorship from TGen scientists as they pursue discoveries about serious illnesses, including neurological conditions, such as Alzheimer's disease, infectious diseases, and many types of cancer. The student scholars also participate in professional development programs in science communication, public speaking, and basic business etiquette.

What about a similar program for students to learn a great deal about education? Substituting the word *education* for hospitals and health care, the foregoing entry for hospitals and health care might read, "The program could involve a great number of teens who are learning more about education and schooling and have the opportunity to work on research and creative projects, escort parents, perform teaching and administrative duties, work alongside staff who mentor them and more." Such an experience for students is not viewed as an internship but rather as a learning experience that encompasses a perspective above and beyond the more singular focus of one teacher in the classroom.

A Model for Improving Preparation Programs for Educational Personnel

The following information sets forth a selected number of curricular course areas that are provided in many local public schools. For example, most secondary public schools offer courses related to business enterprises including typing, shorthand, accounting, business management, and others.

Business Enterprises: typing, shorthand, accounting, business management, business practices, business law, foundations of business, computer applications, computer programming, and others.

Communications: tv applications, speech, English composition, English grammar, foreign languages, and others.

Medical Practice: health and safety, chemistry, psychology, environmental science, biology, health, physical education, and others.

Engineering: physics, algebra, calculus, geometry, trigonometry, industrial arts, and others.

Vocational Education: industrial arts, mechanical drawing, printing, auto mechanics, home economics, electronics, auto body works, carpentry, and others.

Government Services: civics, American history, world history, government, social studies, and others.

Fine Arts: music, orchestra, art, drama, theatre, dance, and others.

What about the Profession of Education as Part of a School's Curricular Program?

A student has one primary source for knowing something about the teaching profession. Unless he or she has a relative in education, commonly he or she relies on what he or she has experienced as a student. We submit that the profession of education should be part of the school curriculum and underscore its vital importance for sustaining a democratic republic government, serving a free enterprise system that continues to improve the standard of living for America's citizens, and providing for the expansion of personal opportunities for each and every individual.

What cognitive and affective characteristics are required for having a successful career in the field of education? What opportunities does a career in education provide for the individual to use personal talents and contribute to the high purposes and values that are required in America? How can you tell a great teacher or a great school administrator when you see one? How does the teacher provide an example of the high values and characteristics admired by the American citizenry? Who is more available and most knowledgeable about answering such questions that the best educational professionals currently in practice?

Keys to the Identification of Great Teachers

For the purposes of identifying, recruiting, and hiring high-quality teachers, school personnel directors must be knowledgeable of the cognitive and affective characteristics of great teachers. Fortunately, there are some studies that have focused on the attributes most commonly demonstrated by effective teachers. For example, in one study of teachers in preparation programs, secondary school students and teacher educators were asked to identify attributes of effective teachers (Adeosun et al. 2013). Twenty-seven characteristics were listed by the study participants, which included "skillful/teaches well" as the leading attribute with a 12.2 percent response. "Kindness" received a response of 9.95 percent, "intelligence" 8.97 percent, "friendliness" with social skills and good interpersonal relations 7.66 percent, and "counselor" skills received 7.66 percent.

Other highly rated attributes of high-quality teachers commonly reported in a variety of studies include such affective skills as caring/loving, positive classroom climate, effective communication skills, enthusiasm, fairness, sense of humor, and good listener. High-level cognitive skills of effective teachers commonly include teacher knowledge, high expectations/standards, command of the field, teacher preparation and credentials, organization, effective teaching strategies, monitoring of student learning, and motivation of students.

The foregoing findings relative to effective teachers can be utilized in several ways, including the drafting of position qualifications for hiring purposes, interviewing observations/questioning, and composition of references. Knowledge of such positive traits serves as "look fors" when drafting position descriptions, asking for references, and evaluating a potential hire's credentials and interview observances. A bad hire will result as one of the school district's biggest mistakes. Nevertheless, the hiring of high-quality teachers and administrative personnel is problematic without the necessary changes in the ways educators are compensated, assigned, and allowed to utilize their own creative talents as professionals.

Teacher Preparation Programming

Investigations reveal the sad results of having aspiring teachers and administrative personnel being prepared "online" or assigned to a local school that has questionable rankings relative to quality programming and student achievement. Prospective teachers should have the most experienced/successful instructors and mentors available. Unfortunately, this is not always the case. University personnel, more commonly, have limited experience in quality education programs at the local school level. One university preparation program, for example, was seeking students who could receive administrative licensure online. Such unfortunate routes for receiving administrative degrees are increasing and, as a result, the quality of administrative talent continues to diminish.

In discussing the current issues facing improvements in educational leadership additionally, we gained permission to quote verbatim the work of Norton (2015) set forth in the publication, *The Changing Landscape of School Leadership: Recalibrating the School Principalship*. This work underscores five major factors that are inhibiting the major improvements needed in administrator training nationally. The detailed discussion of current issues/problems is followed by a rethinking of programs for administrative training.

Included in the current issues facing improvements in education are the following:

1. Institutions of higher education and their presidents are continually striving to become rated as research #1 universities. The #1 rating is primarily based on the institution's record of research grants/funding received by the university's colleges and departments. Science programs, law schools, medical schools, and other colleges that have extraordinary records of grant approvals are prized. Since education colleges are low on the listing of grant funds received, they are given little preference when budgetary cuts are being considered.

Since online degree programs compete favorably with other "degree mills" and do bring in increased enrollment monies, they become popular for that reason alone. The losers are revealed in K–12 school programs that rely on the leadership of school principals and other quality administrative personnel to meet the challenges of today's ever-changing school environment. The higher education persons pushing these programs seldom have experience in K–12 education and commonly are limited in administration experience at that level as well.

2. Farkas et al. (2003) conducted a survey of educational leaders several years ago. At that time, nearly 70 percent of the participants expressed the opinion that traditional leadership programs were "out of touch" with the realities of what it takes to run schools. Another early study (Hale and Moorman 2003) concluded that "principals across the nation argue that administrator training programs deserve an 'F'" (5). These conclusions were stated more than a decade ago and still remain pertinent in the minds of a majority of practicing school leaders.

3. Rather than witnessing program improvements for administrator training, preparation programs have gone soft. One major university in the southwest region of the United States awards its master's degree in educational administration to all potential administrators online. One recruiting ad opens with the statement, "Become a school principal online!" It is not uncommon to have online degree programs in administration supervised by individuals without experience in administration or without degrees with majors in that field.

Most departments of administration have reduced and/or eliminated the requirements of candidate admission testing. Those program applicants with an undergraduate GPA lower than 3.5 in some cases are required to receive a "B+" grade average in their first two graduate courses. Grades less than a "B" are seldom seen in administrative graduate programs.

4. Departments of administration with the titles of Educational Administration and Supervision have given way to titles such as The Department of Research and Policy Studies. Yet serious attention to research tends to be missing. One-year residency requirements for doctoral degree students and full-time administrative internships are becoming things of the past. The department director of one program that housed educational administration, higher education, community education, and policy studies held a doctorate in English. The director had never been a teacher or administrator in a public or private K–12 educational program. Under this "leadership," the department of educational administration and higher education collapsed and ultimately was dissolved. What took its place? An online master's degree program was instituted that resulted in licensure for all administrative positions in elementary, middle, and secondary schools.

5. What about residency requirements or administrative internship requirements?

Several contacts with university officials gave us this norm. A doctoral student must take a minimum of nine semester hours during one semester to meet the residency requirements. That is, the candidate must take a three-semester credit course in the fall, winter, and summer terms to meet the residency requirements. A freshman college student surpasses such a flawed doctoral residency requirement. Full-time involvement in the study of educational administration or a full-time internship in educational administration is a thing of the past. In most programs, a comprehensive examination is required followed by a defense of a major research study. The overall result is a licensed school administrator unprepared to meet effectively the issues and problems that are encountered in the school principalship today.

Let's compare the foregoing preparation requirements with that of a doctoral graduate from a U.S. or Canadian medical school. The graduate must have attended four full terms of instruction of eight months each, with all courses having been completed by physical on-site attendance in the country in which the school is chartered. The requirement of four full terms of instruction for eight months may be waived for any applicant for licensure who has graduated from an international school of medicine, has substantially complied with the attendance requirements provided herein, and is certified by a specialty board recognized by the American Board of Medical Specialties (ABMS) or the American Osteopathic Association's Bureau of Osteopathic Specialists (AOA-BOS).

Some of the specific requirements for international medical school graduates are as follows: must have attained the MD, DO, or MBBS degree; must have completed four full years of medical school consisting of eight months each, with all courses having been completed by physical on-site attendance in the country in which the school is chartered; must have passed the ECFMG, ULMLE, NBME, and LMCC exams or an acceptable combination of the exams in accordance with the state's administrative rules; must have completed three years of clinical-based postgraduate training in the United States or Canada in an accredited training program in more than two specialties.

Comparing doctoral preparation programs in education to medical doctor programs does appear to be stretching the point. Nevertheless, the preparation of educational leaders is failing in many respects. Personnel preparation has to get much better; doing the same thing and decreasing the preparation program requirements for aspiring educational leaders will not quiet the loud voices being directed to what a large percentage of practicing educators view as a failing preparation program.

More Out of the Proverbial Box Thinking: Changes for Preparation Programs

Online degree programs for licensing teachers and school administrators and having them "trained" on school sites that are failing to provide high-quality education programs must be discontinued. University programs, as such, are not meeting the preparation requirements. Unless we become more able to recruit and enroll the most capable human resources for educational leadership, the thoughts of major improvement in preparation programs most likely will remain as an unfulfilled hope. The vision and program plans are to implement a preparation program that inspires talented personnel to enter the education profession and then to expand continuously their knowledge and skills for administering changes that result in meaningful improvements in student learning.

Consider the recent report by Harris (2018) relative to how one online charter school reportedly is using its annual $30 million state funding. According to the report, less than a quarter of the students passed the math and about a third passed the English on the state's standardized tests; both were below state standards. Student dropout rate was reported as 49 percent. However, the most troublesome report of the school's activities is that beginning in 2012, making money became the school's primary activity. Reportedly, more than $30 million state allotment was not spent on instruction; rather, it was spent on stocks, bonds, mortgage-backed securities, and real estate. To top it all, Harris reported that the school's founder and chief executive later received $8.8 million a payment that exceeded by $4 million the combined compensation of the school's ninety-four teachers.

Such a payment was thirty-nine times the salary of the superintendent of schools in the largest or second largest school district in the state. The school enrollment in the charter school in question is less than one-third the enrollment of the school district just mentioned. The politics of the case herein is reported in some depth by Harris in the September 7, 2018 issue of the *Arizona Republic*.

Our vision then is to plan and implement a preparation program that inspires talented personnel to enter the educational profession and then to expand continuously their knowledge and skills for administering changes that result in meaningful improvements in student learning. In the following section, we capitalize on the work of Norton in relation to his detailed explanation of a model preparation program as set forth in his publication, *The Changing Landscape of School Leadership* (2015). Permission has been granted by Rowman & Littlefield to describe the preparation model in its full detail.

The model is universal in the sense that it fits and meets the program needs of each state and their higher and local school education goals and objectives. Its importance is vested in its pronouncement of major changes in identifying and recruiting highly talented individuals to the career of education and ultimately leadership positions in local school communities.

First and foremost is the paramount need for reducing the number of institutions that are in the "business" of preparing school leaders. Far too many institutions that claim to be preparing school leaders are unqualified and undermanned to implement this important program at a high-quality level. A policy for implementing and controlling an administrator preparation program must be passed by the state legislature and policies for its implementation adopted by each state's board of education led by a state superintendent of schools. If the proliferation of ineffective "programs of preparation" is permitted to continue, the improvement of quality educational leadership will remain as only a wish.

The information below sets forth early programs for fostering career interests in education.

Career/Occupational/Business Programs for Public Schools

Importance of Education in America
How Education Promotes the Standards of Living for All Americans
School Visitations
The Opportunities for Teaching and Leading in Education
What Is School Administration?
The Education Club for Students
Student Observations, "Teaching" Activities

Entering Higher Education to Earn a BSEd

- Assessment/Evaluation Requirements
- Residency (on-site program relationships/experiences in recognized high-performing schools)
- Admission Testing:
  - GPA and Other Test Scores
  - SAT Scores
  - ACT Score
- Related Education Knowledge:
  - Reading
  - Mathematics
  - Science
  - Writing/Composition
  - English Grammar
  - Development General Studies
- Development of Education Program of Studies
- Degree Specialization
- On-Site Teaching Experiences

Entering Graduate Education in a State-Approved Education Academy for a Master's Degree Program of Studies in Educational Administration/Teaching Media

- Core Courses in Educational Administration or Teaching
- Curriculum and Supervision Specialty
- Learning Leadership

- Finance/Business Specialty
- Student Advocacy
- Technology in the Educational Program
- Human Resources Administration
- School Climate and Student Achievement
- Assistant School Principal Component
- On-Site Internships
- Research Applications
- Residency Year Experiences
- One-Year Residency Administrator License

Entering Administrator Academy for Approved Doctoral Administration Program of Studies Sponsored by the State Legislature

- One-Year Specialty Program to Earn the Administrative License for the Position of Assistant Principal
- Two-Year Specialty Program to Earn the Administrative License for School Principal
- Three-Year Specialty Program to Earn the Administrative License for the School Superintendency
- Expenses for each License Program Is Paid by the Federal and State Agencies Courses:
  - Politics and Power Structure
  - Coaching and Mentoring
  - Leadership
  - Business and Finance
  - School Climate and Student Achievement
  - Achievement Assessment and Evaluation
  - On-Site Internships
  - Communication Strategies
  - Selected Studies (as fits the case)
  - The Administrator as Consumer, Dispenser, and Implementer of Research

Professional Development Program Requirements Completed at and/or under the Supervision of the Administrators' Educational Academy

- Each Administrative License Is Renewed Every Three Years by Attending Academy Courses, Workshops, and Special Research Programs

- Administrator Licensing Based on Demonstrated Knowledge and Competence of Administrative Requirements as Opposed to Course Credits
- An Approved Academy and/or Other Highly Qualified Person Is Appointed as a Mentor for Academy Graduates: Group Mentoring Services Are Ongoing
- Required Improvement Plans Are Monitored by Academy Personnel

The preparation model is designed to foster three primary purposes:

1. Fostering the interest of young people in education through planned programs that underscore the important opportunities that it provides and encouraging talented young children and youth to participate in educational activities similar to what one might do relative to an early interest in nursing, law, or business enterprise.

2. Upgrading the preparation of educational leadership programs toward the goal of promoting visionary leadership attitudes accompanied by extensive knowledge and experience that focus on leadership; for positive development for all school leaders.

3. Reemphasizing the paramount importance of educational support by all local, state, and federal agencies for establishing a financial support structure for education that ensures the attraction of high-quality personnel into the career field of education and educational administration.

Does the foregoing administrative model require more time for administrator preparation and licensing? The answer is yes. Is the model more expensive for the participants? The answer is most likely yes. However, some aspects of the degree programs must be subsidized by state and federal agencies. Education's local, state, and national significance requires that it be given priority for financial support.

Educational Research: The *Sine Qua Non* of Being the Best of All Worlds

Try to picture the status of the medical profession, technological progress, or business enterprises without the results of ongoing, valid, and reliable research. If, for example, a cure for Alzheimer's disease were discovered, its application into medical practice would be immediate and worldwide. Yet, the few important research findings in education relative to student retention, class size, learning styles, and school climate have had little or no effect on contemporary practices. Education goes on doing the same thing as before.

We contend that, unless quality research is implemented for education practices at the national, state, and local levels, the thought of education as being the best of all worlds will remain unfulfilled. Give a moment's thought to the schools to which you are or have been familiar. How many of them had a viable research program that focused on educational practices and then had their results implemented in meeting educational improvements?

The reference here is not a research office that keeps a record of enrollment projections, dropout statistics, test scores, and such. Rather, educational research is considered to be the central core of school program decisions including curriculum development, student learning standards, pilot program outcomes, results of curriculum interventions, assessments of financial support, and other interventions that focus on effects of present and projected program strategies.

A recent meeting at a major university in one state centered on the topic of reimagining teacher and administrator preparation programs. After spending the lion's share of the discussion on how the university is working on reimagining program planning and implementation in K–12 schools, one attendant asked the question, "Just what is the status of the university's research activities relative to what is being implemented at the local school level?" The reply, "That's a good question and something that we have been thinking about for sometime now." In other words, the university officials had done nothing in regard to researching the program changes being promoted for local schools to adopt or how the implemented changes were to be validated by effective research activities.

Some university preparation degree programs already have reduced the research requirements for licensing school leaders. Instead, emphasis is being directed to on-site practice activities with report-backed experience papers. As one university veteran professor stated in one of our visitations, "As far as research knowledge and skills go, at present our students don't know the difference between a research hypothesis and a manhole cover." Although it is troublesome to talk about the status of research competency in contemporary educational preparation programs, research knowledge and skills have lessened rather than increased in most preparation programs. As previously stated, valid and reliable research program activities that reach the local school programs are the sine qua non of positive change in the quality and equity of public school education in America.

Take any or all research activities away from the medical profession or other technical professions that have resulted in significant improvements for America's citizens and living standards would suffer immensely. One of the U.S. government's most significant contributions to public school education would be to support the implementation of an effective educational research component within each state and local school district in America. Too costly? Perhaps, but not as costly as not doing so.

We have contended throughout this chapter that the lack of a comprehensive research program in education is the basic reason that so many programs and change interventions are implemented and then tend to fade away. No newly implemented change seems to work for any long period of time. As stated by Norton, "We give high hopes for the advancement of educational research in the reimagination of school programs nationally. If, indeed, new roles, programs and procedures are to be implemented, not only is the procedure of planning of primary importance, but ongoing assessment strategies and team-based research must accompany it" (2018, xx). It is clear that very few, if any, preparation programs are presently ready to assume such an important research objective.

Local school principals and instructional personnel must become users, dispensers, and implementers of quality educational research. Such a viable research program within a school district will require highly qualified personnel. Are these kinds of talents presently available for leading such a program? If so, how are they to be attracted to education? How are they to be supported? How prepared are local school districts to implement effective research to support ongoing action research that serves to determine if program purposes are actually being achieved? We contend that answers to these kinds of questions are of paramount importance if, indeed, education in America is to be the best of all worlds.

The important initiation of a research climate at the local school level could begin with the implementation of action research. Action research appears to fit well with reimagining in relation to its view of the collaborative procedures carried out by those professionals with a shared educational concern. Such a collaborative research effort serves to develop a systematic, inquiring approach toward a team's own practices and to make a positive change in what the team has been doing. Reimagination changes/improvements will only succeed if they are accompanied by effective ongoing research results.

Action research is not a new entry for consideration. Rather, it represents one of education's seldom used strategies for educational improvement. Sagor's book, *Guiding School Improvement with Action Research* (2000), points out that action research can be initiated by a single teacher, a group of teachers with similar interests, or by the entire faculty of a school for improving and/or refining the teacher's instructional strategies.

As stated by Sagor (2000), "The reality is that our public schools will not prevail with the challenges . . . unless they encourage experimentation, inquiry, and dialogue by those pioneers (the teachers) who are working toward meeting those challenges. For this reason, it is imperative that these twenty-first century pioneers, our classroom teachers, conduct the research 'standards attainment' themselves" (7).

Overtime, numerous articles have been published on the topic of action research. It is beyond this chapter to give the full details of action research procedures and strategies. However, every reference to action research underscores the importance of having the teacher or group of teachers determine what area(s) of instruction need the most attention and which ones benefit student learning. This important beginning is commonly referred to as the *focus* of the action research.

The steps of initiating and carrying out the action research project is much the same as any other research model. After determining the purposes of the research and specifying the questions to be answered, the gathering of related data, the evaluation and assessment of that data, the conclusions that result from the data assessment, communication of the research results, and finally implementing the study results are followed. Implementation of the results, especially if it has implications for all teachers, is communicated and developed as fits the case. In addition, and of paramount importance, is the initiation of a plan to monitor and evaluate the change in question.

POST-CHAPTER QUIZ

Directions: For each multiple-choice question, circle the best or correct answer. Refrain from just guessing the answer, rather just move to the next question. Check your answers with the correct answers and brief discussions at the end of the quiz.

1. According to one report on school funding, what percentage of public school funding is paid by the federal government nationally?

   a. 10 percent
   b. 20 percent
   c. 30 percent
   d. 40 percent
   e. 50 percent or higher

2. The terms "reimagining" and "change," as they apply to education program practices, are

   a. virtually synonymous.
   b. terms referring to visionary interventions.
   c. different in their meaning.
   d. terms that entered the scientific management era in the early 1900s.
   e. terms primarily credited to the progressive movement in education.

3. What percentage of teachers nationally leave the profession after their first year?

    a. 10 percent
    b. 20 percent
    c. 30 percent
    d. 40 percent
    e. 50 percent or higher

4. *The Rodriquez v. State of Texas* court ruling stated that

    a. the drafters of the U.S. Constitution erred in not mentioning education in the document.
    b. every child in every school is guaranteed an equal opportunity to education.
    c. every child is not guaranteed an equal opportunity to education.
    d. only the states have the responsibility to make a decision on equity of education.
    e. None of the above.

5. The U.S. government has used what federal document to justify its entry into matters of public education?

    a. The U.S. Constitution
    b. The Tenth Amendment to the Constitution
    c. A court ruling of *Jefferson v. the Gov. of Maryland*
    d. The Twenty-Eighth Amendment to the Constitution
    e. The preamble to the U.S. Constitution

6. This chapter stresses the fact that valid and reliable research methods are

    a. being emphasized in virtually every preparation program for educational leaders.
    b. being viewed as less important in virtually every program for educational leaders.
    c. being "softened" in preparation programs for school leaders.
    d. becoming the common core topics for programs in administrative preparation.
    e. None of the above.

7. Which condition is the one most commonly related to the concept of a national curriculum?

    a. Every state-funded school must offer a curriculum that is balanced and broadly based.

b. A national curriculum forms only one part of the local school curriculum.
c. Only ungraded forms of school organization are permitted in any public school.
d. Teacher licensure shall be determined by the U.S. Office of Education.
e. None of the above.

8. It has been found that the ability to fund education differs among the states in a ratio of

   a. 2 to 1
   b. 3 to 1
   c. 4 to 1
   d. 5 to 1
   e. 6 to 1

9. For the purposes of identifying, recruiting, and hiring high-quality teachers, personnel directors must

   a. be highly qualified teachers themselves.
   b. have administrative experience.
   c. have at least five years of teaching experience.
   d. be knowledgeable about the cognitive and affective characteristics of great teachers.
   e. rely primarily on evidence gathered from the university personnel supervisors.

10. Implementation of courses within the public schools that center on education and its purposes and opportunities has been

    a. ruled unlawful by the courts.
    b. ruled as "self-interest" by the courts.
    c. dropped in most cases in public schools due to the lack of qualified personnel to teach such courses.
    d. given little or no serious consideration by public school personnel.
    e. None of the above.

11. A major component missing in the majority of public schools is

    a. parental involvement.
    b. effective professional development.
    c. salaries based on time in-service.
    d. a research component.
    e. None of the above.

12. One specific characteristic of action research is that it can be implemented and carried out

    a. by unbiased persons outside the school operations.
    b. by a single teacher.
    c. with zero expenses.
    d. by the school support staff.
    e. None of the above.

13. The primary goal of this chapter is

    a. to demonstrate the fact that educational personnel are teachers and administrators and not research experts.
    b. to inform the reader that education is being underfunded.
    c. to enhance the understanding that the financial issues facing education in America and the personnel issues facing education must be resolved before quality education can be assured.
    d. to recommend more research courses to preparation programs for aspiring school administrators.
    e. to stress the fact that preparation programs for school leaders must be reimagined and much improved.

DISCUSSION OF THE POST-CHAPTER QUIZ

Question #1

The answer to question #1, the percentage of education funding by the federal government, is "a," "10 percent." Although, different information sources state that the federal portion of educational funding is 8 to 10 percent. It depends on the extent that the federal government is including educational expenditures. Is it for K–12 public schools only? Or, does the funding include funding for higher education, vocational education, prekindergarten programs, and private/charter schools? In any case 10 percent for the federal government, 45 percent for the state, and 45 percent for the local school district is a fairly accurate account of public school funding in America.

Question #2

The answer to question #2 is "c," "different in their meaning." The term *change* means to make something different as to undergo a modification in present procedures. The term *reimagining* means to form a new conception or to recreate a completely new practice or way of doing things.

Question #3

The answer to question #3 is either "b" or "c," "20 percent" or "30 percent." Actually, the first-year loss most commonly is stated as being 20 to 30 percent. Most any loss of teacher personnel is problematic, but empirical evidence indicates that a large number of the one-year losses is the school district's best teachers. Over a five-year time period, research evidence shows that 50 percent of a group of teachers who enter the profession leave by the fifth year of their teaching experience.

Question #4

The answer to question #4 is "c," every child is not guaranteed an equal education by the Rodriquez ruling of the U.S. Supreme Court. This is why the answer to the question as to whether public education is a right or a privilege most commonly is ruled to be a privilege. In any case, the *Rodriquez v. The State of Texas* ruling has had major implications for educational practices within the states.

Question #5

The answer to question #5 is "e," "the preamble to the Constitution." It states, "We the people of the United States in order to form a more perfect union, establish justice, insure domestic tranquility, provide for the common defense, *promote the general welfare,* and secure the Blessings of Liberty to ourselves and prosperity, do ordain and establish the Constitution for the United States of America." The phrase, *promote the general welfare*, has been used to justify the federal government entry into such local school programs as serving the special needs of handicapped children, vocational education, special education, school lunch programs, and other such interventions.

Question #6

The answers to question #6 are both "b" and "c." That is, such requirements for research studies at the close of the master's degree program, the dropping of the requirement of a major dissertation for doctoral degrees, and attention to the need for practicing school leaders to be developers, implementers, and dispensers of quality research in preparation/degree programs are lessening in preparation programs nationally. Research knowledge and skill are being replaced with onsite administrative activities.

Question #7

The answer to question #7 is "b," "a national curriculum forms only one part of the local school's curricular program. Although a national curriculum does focus on the desired aims, purposes, and goals of the school curriculum, theoretically, the administration of the curriculum is left to the state and local school districts. It is reasonable to assume that a national school curriculum would result in more control of the public school programs at the local school level.

Question #8

The answer to question #8 is "e," "6 to 1." That is, the property values available for tax income in the richest states are six times higher than states with the lowest values. In fact, one single neighborhood property in New York was more valuable than the entire property of five states in the United States. This difference, of course, is a primary reason for educational inequities and opportunities for students in several states. Efforts to insure educational equity is a continuing issue/problem in America.

Question #9

The answer to question #9 is "d," "be knowledgeable about the affective and cognitive and affective characteristics of great teachers." Such knowledge serves the personnel director and others in several positive ways. For instance, such information helps in drafting position job descriptions, developing job interview questions, gathering references, and determining the kinds of data that need to be gathered on each job applicant.

Question #10

The answer to question #10 is "d," "given little or no serious consideration by public school personnel." This chapter has favored the teaching of the importance of education for retaining a democratic nation, promoting the continuation of a free enterprise system in the country, and providing each individual a fair start and equal chance in the race of life. A high-quality education within the nation results in a benefit to all citizens; the standards of living increase in a positive fashion when the citizenry is knowledgeable and productive.

Question #11

The answer to question #11 is "d," "a research component." It has been contended that an effective research culture within the school district is the sine qua non to a best of all worlds result. Erase all of the results from the medical profession and the profession would be set back enormously. This chapter has underscored the need for research programs to be extended throughout the educational profession. Education's future depends on it.

Question #12

The answer to question #12 is "b," it can be carried out "by a single teacher." Although a related group of professional teachers can collaborate in carrying out a project of action research, a single teacher can focus on one aspect of his or her instruction and set up a basic action research plan to check on an instructional area of concern. The teacher does the planning and the teacher implements the research plan. It is the teacher who benefits from the results but the results are most likely information that other colleagues will benefit from as well.

Question #13

The answer to question #13 is "c," "to enhance the understanding that the financial issues facing education in America and the personnel issues must be resolved before the best of the world's education can be assured." This chapter has not resolved the financial question regarding education in America. However, more money and a reimagination of many aspects of public education are crucial if such a realization is to be achieved. As popular as is the federal government's involvement in public school education, additional federal government funding appears to be the *sine quo non* of the best of all world's aim for public education in America.

Key Chapter Ideas and Recommendations

- Throughout the history of education, thousands of words have been written concerning the "failures" in education including the crucial need for a much higher level of financial support. In the world of reality, it has been much easier to criticize education's failures than to recommend and/ or develop viable solutions. Equity for one school district tends to result in inequity for others. One contemporary "push" for educational financial support is termed the Robinhood Concept or tax the rich to give to the poor. We contend that this position is another unacceptable and fleeting solution.

- If education is not given high priority in relation to financial support, education will continue to be less than the best of the world.

- The federal government has relied on the Preamble to the U.S. Constitution for its "authority" to intervene into the affairs of public school education. Such involvement focuses on the welfare clause to "mandate" what it believes to be in the best interests of the nation.

- The solution to the financial funding problems of public education appears to rest outside the proverbial box of educational thought. Nevertheless, such thinking might be just what is needed. The chapter attempts to emphasize the many concepts that ultimately became major positive solutions to ideas that were originally viewed as being "impossible."
- Inequity in educational opportunity among the states must become more than something that is just talked about. The problem of inequity must be raised to the top of America's priorities if indeed a financial support resolution is to be found.
- The establishment of educational foundations for resolving education's financial needs problem is flawed.
- The paramount importance of education for America's sustaining of a democratic form of government, support of a free enterprise system, and benefits for each and every citizen is a concept that must be included in public school education programs in grade K–12.
- Efforts to attract, prepare, recruit, and hire highly qualified personnel for positions in education must become a reality that is initiated in the early education programs within public schools.
- Perhaps just putting more money into present education programs is not the answer but more money for attracting high-quality personnel and retaining their services is an important answer to the claims of a "failing education" program in our nation.
- Presently, public school education curriculum gives considerable attention to the opportunities in various professions. Why not a well-planned and required program of education in America for K–12 schoolchildren and youth?
- Teacher and administrator preparation programs must be reimagined so as to prepare the very best persons for positions in education. The present practice of outsourcing preparation activities is flawed in many ways. When aspiring teachers and administrators are sent to schools that are themselves failing in many respects, positive outcomes are not likely. In addition, school practitioners themselves argue that the administrative training programs that they experienced deserve an "F." This result is unsatisfactory.
- First and foremost, valid and reliable research programs must be initiated at all levels of government, federal, state, and local. The lack of local education research components missing in the large majority of public schools should not be tolerated. From the standpoint of practice, administrative

leaders in education should be knowledgeable and skilled as utilizers, disseminators, and implementers of valid research that focuses on the issues and problems facing the school. It is almost impossible to visualize other important professions and businesses that do not have effective research programs in place.

- The concept of action research holds many benefits for improving teacher performance and learning results for students. Both preparation programs for educational professionals and ongoing professional development activities need to stress the importance of basic and empirical research. Strong research components are missing in the large majority of public school programs. However, such a component should be among the foundation bases for determining the educational programs for children and youth in the nation's public schools.

Discussion Questions

1. Assume that you are chairing a meeting of parents and teachers. One parent asks, "You mentioned the terms reimagining and change. What do these terms mean and what is the difference between them, if any?" What is your response to the question?

2. A teacher at your school asks about applications of action research in the classroom. What applications of action research might you mention? How might the matter of student learning styles be clarified by way of an action research activity in a classroom?

3. Resolution: "Education will not be approved just by adding more money to teachers' salaries." Take either the pro or con position and write your defense to the resolution posed.

4. The primary financial support for public school education comes from local, state, and federal taxes. Presently, the local school district, the state, and the federal government fund approximately 45 percent, 45 percent, and 10 percent, respectively, of public education funding. Using the information gained from this chapter and your own knowledge and opinion about financial support of public education, write one or two pages on how you would recommend that public education funding be improved. Avoid generalizations as much as possible.

5. After completing the requirements set forth in question #4, give serious thought to the ramifications of your recommendations. For example, if you recommend that the federal government's percentage of support be increased, what are the likely ramifications/complaints of what you are recommending?

Case Study
Bad News, Let's Just Roll Up Our Sleeves and Get Back to Work

Principal Watkins opened the meeting of his faculty by stating that he unfortunately had some bad news. In short, the State Department of Education had given the high school a grade of "C" for the year's performance. According to the state assessment report, test scores in mathematics, English composition, and general science were lower than the previous year.

"I guess my recommendation that we place more emphasis on student self-learning didn't pan out as well as I had hoped," said Principal Watkins. "Since I left the definition of self-learning mainly to your discretion, I just assumed that this method would serve to engage students into the learning process."

Principal Watkins paused for a moment and then asked the group if they had any questions about what they had hoped to implement and accomplish this year concerning improvements in student learning.

Art Miller, teacher of mathematics, raised his hand and was recognized by Principal Watkins.

"I just didn't feel comfortable most of the time just assigning a lesson and letting the students work it out themselves. Oh, I was available to help out if a student raised his or her hand, but I don't know, maybe some were just too reluctant to do so."

Miss Woolhether, an English teacher, commented she relied a great deal on the students' completion of the homework assignment. She noted that generally it took her 20 to 30 minutes of class time checking over the homework papers before she could put the class back to work on the next assignment.

Jack Valentiner, a teacher of science, said that he thought the self-learning process went quite well in his general science and biology classes. He noted that student conduct was good and class time seemed to go right by. When the brightest students finished the class project or assignment, Valentiner just asked them to help others who were somewhat struggling.

Principal Watkins informed the faculty members that he was to meet with the assistant superintendent in charge of instruction within the week. He indicated that he would explain that this was the first year with the self-learning strategy and that they would expect improvements next year. He closed the meeting by saying, "Let me know if I can be of service to you in any way."

Case Study Discussion Questions

1. First, write out your thoughts about what took place at the faculty meeting? Give special attention to what you believe the faculty members took away from the session.
2. To what extent do you believe that the faculty understands the instructional methods that principal Watkins has in mind? Or how well does principal Watkins appear to be clear on the so-called self-learning strategy?
3. Take a few minutes to put yourself in the principal's role in this case. Set forth recommendations that you believe are in order in this case?

REFERENCES

Adeosun, E., Oni, S., and Oladipo, B. (2013). "Affective and Cognitive Characteristics of Nigerian Student Teachers: Towards Developing an Effective Teacher Education Framework." *Journal of International Cooperation, CICE Hiroshima University* 15 (3): 39–58.

Biddle, B. J., and Berliner, D. C. (2002). "A Research Synthesis/Unequal School Funding in the United States." *Educational Leadership* 29 (8): 48–59.

Cano, R. (2018a). "State Will Take Over Murphy School District. Financial Woes Lead to Rare Interventions." *Arizona Republic*, June 26.

Department for Education (2013). *The National Curriculum in England: Key Stages 1 and 2 Framework Document, September 2013. Digital Education Resource Archive (DERA)*, last motified September 24. http://dera.ioe.ac.uk/id/eprint/18300.

Farkas, S., Johnson, J., and Duffett, A. (2003). *Rolling Up Their Sleeves: Superintendents and Principals Talk about What's Needed to Fix Public Schools*. New York: Public Agenda.

Hale, E., and Moorman, H. (2003). *Preparing School Principals: A National Perspective on Policy and Program Innovations*. Washington, DC: Institute for Educational Leadership.

Harris, C. (2018). "State Charter Association Adopts Tougher Ethics Policy after Republic reports inside deal." *Arizona Republic*, September 7. https://www.azcentral.com/story/news/local/arizona-education/2018/09/07/arizona-charter-schools-association-adopts-tougher-ethics-policy-local-education/1215176002/.

Kowai, J., and Thomas, D. J. (2002). "What's Right with Public Education. Fastback 501." *ERIC*. ED478534. Bloomington, IN: Phi Delta Kappa Educational Foundation.

Kumar, H. (2014). "10 Ways to Make the Impossible Possible!" *Launch Your Genius* (blog), November 11. launchyourgenius.com/2014/11/11/impossible/.

New, B. (2012). "Key to Public Funding? How about Foundations?" (op-ed). *PennLive,* February 10. https://www.pennlive.com/editorials/index.ssf/2012/02/key_to_public_school_funding_h.html.

Norton, M. S. (2015). *The Changing Landscape of School Leaders: Recalibrating the School Principalship*. Lanham, MD: Rowman & Littlefield.

Norton, M. S. (2017). *Guiding the Human Resources Function in Education: New Issues, New Needs*. Lanham, MD: Rowman & Littlefield.

Sagor, R. (2000). *What Is Action Research? Guiding School Improvement with Action Research*. Alexandria, VA: Association for Supervision and Curriculum Development.

Semuels, Alana. (2016). "Good School, Rich School; Bad School, Poor School: The Inequality at the Heart of America's Education System." *The Atlantic*, August 25. https://www.theatlantic.com/business/archive/2016/08/property-taxes-and-unequal-schools/497333/.

Satell, G. (2015). "How the Impossible Becomes Possible." *Forbes,* June 20. https://www.forbes.com/sites/gregsatell/2015/06/20/how-the-impossible-becomes-possible/#2cf2979f3d70.

USA Today Network (2018). "High School Volunteers Learning Medical Field." *Arizona Republic*, July 20, Tempe-Ahwatukee, Z10.

Yozwiak, S. (2018). "Southeast Valley Students Graduate from Helios scholars' Program at TGen." Tempe-Ahwatukee-USA Today Network. Special to the *Arizona Republic*, July 29, Z10.

Chapter 3

Social Issues and the Importance of Public Education for Dealing with Them

The primary chapter goal: To examine and analyze the matter of purposes of education with special attention being given to social issues and their impact on educational programming, curricular debates, and ultimately student learning. Emphasis is given to the vital importance of special programs for extending the services for the mental and physical health of all students in America's schools.

AMERICA'S SOCIAL ISSUES AND THE EXTENT TO WHICH EDUCATION IS RESPONSIBLE FOR DEALING WITH THEM

The problems and issues that the nation is encountering presently weigh heavily upon education and the considerations related to public education's ability to succeed. The social issues embedded in America's environments are present in school settings across the country. Consider the social issue of severe poverty. Statistical reports and definitions of poverty widely differ in regard to its status in the United States. How poverty is determined and the living conditions of "poverty" families are controversial. The entire space reserved for this chapter could be used to discuss poverty and its negative impact on public school programs. We contend that major innovations are needed in the social issues facing the nation. The issues permeate public education and must be resolved if education indeed is to be the best of all worlds.

Education's focus on educational purposes has varied historically as it is influenced by the social environment in which it operates and the pressures placed upon it to improve students' academic knowledge and skills in order to compete technically with other world nations. In the following section, several social issues are set forth for consideration. The reader's opinion as to the implications of each issue for the public school's responsibility is solicited. In each case, you are asked to rank the listed issue as being of high concern or low concern for contemporary public schools. That is, should the public school be directly involved in the education issue set forth?

At the outset, we ask you to give thought to the following listing of current national/school social issues (table 3.1). Second, you are asked to give your opinion as to the importance of each issue for local public schools. Should the public school be responsible for helping to resolve the social issues that pervade the school-community, state, and nation? Is such an issue one that public schools must aim to improve?

Many schools nationally are dealing with these social issues in various ways. At this point in the discussion, the purpose is to underscore these issues and the fact that each one has implications for affecting school program practices and student achievement results. The federal government has ruled that public schools must be open to every child regardless of their special needs. Programs for special needs students have improved greatly within the past several years. In the early 1960s, for example, few school districts had

Table 3.1 Social issues facing schools in America. According to your opinion, rate the seriousness of the issue and level of the school's responsibility for "resolving it," wherein 5 = highest and 1 = lowest.

Social Issue	Seriousness of the Issue for Education	A Matter for Education to Help Resolve
Severe poverty		
Homelessness		
Teenage parenting		
Alcohol and drugs		
Bullying and cyberbullying		
Violence and vandalism		
School dropouts		
Child abuse and neglect		
Adolescent suicide		
Latch-key children		
Health and safety needs		
Racism		
Teenage pregnancy		
Mental health and anxiety		
Gangs		

comprehensive programs for special education students. Today, student disabilities have been identified increasingly and provisions for them within the school environment have improved.

Yet, along with the gaining of knowledge concerning educational deficiencies, finding the ways to deal with them is often an insurmountable task. Table 3.2 sets forth selected student disabilities and school services that are present in the majority of contemporary schools. The indication of student disabilities goes far beyond the concept of programs for slow learners only.

The Status of Special Needs Provisions in School Districts Nationally

The failing mark pasted on schools today tends to focus on standardized test results in academic subjects of reading, mathematics, English, and science. Although standardized tests on such areas as critical thinking and U.S. history

Table 3.2 Selected Student Disabilities and Student Services

Student Disabilities	Student Special Services
Physically disabled	Evaluation and special services
Attention-deficit disorder	Mobility services
Neurological impairments	Home and hospital services
Serious emotional disturbances	Occupational therapy
Speech and language disturbances	Parent counseling/training
Orthopedic impairments	Psychological services
Autism/pervasive development disorder	Referral services
Asperger's syndrome	Social work services
Bipolar disorder	Therapeutic recreation
Blind and visual impairment	Medical diagnostic services
Cerebral palsy	Home schooling
Chronic health problems	
Deaf and hearing impairment	
Mental retardation	
Dyslexia	
Economic disadvantage	
Homelessness	
Multi-handicapped student	
Learning disabilities	
Learning disabled/gifted student	
Tourette syndrome	
Dysgraphia	
Dyspraxia	
ADD/ADHD (attention disorders)	

Source: M. S. Norton, L. Kelly, and A. Battle (2012). *The Principal as Student Advocate: A Guide to Doing What's Best for All Students*. Lanham, MD: Rowman & Littlefield.

have been administered to some extent, there has not been a significant standardized test on social matters for determining students' awareness of the consequences of negative social issues. Yet, the effects of social issues on school program instruction and student achievement are overwhelming according to school principals and teachers.

As reported by Anderson and Cardoza (2016), 20 percent of children living in America show signs or symptoms of mental health problems. Theoretically, five students in a class of twenty-five have problems with such disabilities as depression, anxiety, substance abuse, and others that result in major problems for education including low academic achievement, absenteeism, problematic behavior, and ultimately dropping out of school altogether.

The question that remains is: How well prepared are America's local public schools to help out with such issues? Many schools face the lack of human and material resources to deal sufficiently with these major disabilities, and so such problems often go undetected and thus uncared for. Providing the necessary human and material resources for dealing with these kinds of social issues will necessitate additional human and financial resources that are readily available to all local schools. The complexity of this need is far-reaching. There are major questions concerning the status of public schools today being able to deal with them effectively. The need for special human resources presently is far out of the reach of education's budgetary allocations. In reality, what we have in mind would not only increase the payment allocations required from the state and local taxes but would also more than double the federal financial support provided at this time in our history.

The Story of Thelma

Thelma was seldom called upon by her teachers since she seldom was paying attention to what was being discussed in class. She seldom was able to follow directions even though the teacher had explained them previously. The lack of organization was evident in her efforts to complete a given task and her responses to a question or task at hand were more "off the cuff" than well thought out in any logical fashion. Her inability to complete a task was troublesome, and she never seemed to be able to get started on a task, which led to criticisms by her teachers of laziness, apathy, and negative attitude.

There was the true case of Thelma. She went through the grades missing letters when reading or not being able to read at all. She went through the grades on the basis of "just passing" and ultimately graduated from high school. She was mostly viewed as a loner, no real friends, and never elected to any school committee or office. She simply tolerated school.

Years later, as an adult, Thelma became especially efficient as a foster mother and supportive community member. Thelma met with her high school classmates at a school reunion years later. As she introduced herself once again to her former classmates at the reunion, she commented as follows: "As a student in high school I realize that everyone thought that I was just stupid. I found out later that I had dyslexia that interfered with my ability to read, write and spell." If Thelma had been able to have the support services that many effective schools have today, she would have had the needed help much earlier and her early life would have been positive as it should be for all students.

A common treatment for dyslexia is tutoring and using apt educational approaches and techniques. A common treatment is termed *multisensory instruction*, which uses structured language education (MDLE). Teachers who are helping kids with dyslexia might use sandpaper letters to learn phonics and spelling or they might learn syllables by tapping them out with their fingers. What does this discussion and others have to do with school practices for dealing with social issues? The answer is everything!

More and more of the student disabilities are being found in school classrooms to be "resolved" by the classroom teacher or specialist in the school district. Yet, the time given to improve dyslexia and other social problems "takes away" from the time and resources needed for academic subjects for children and youth not troubled with such problems. More teachers, more specialists, more facilities, and more money are required. It isn't only the concern that some states' school districts cannot afford the extension of such program provisions. The truth of the matter is that public school education cannot afford not to afford such services.

It has been estimated that only 40 percent of students with emotional, behavioral, and mental health disorders graduate from high school. This percentage is the highest dropout rate of any disabilities group. What kinds of human resources are most commonly required to deal with special needs cases? They often require the services of members of the family, the teacher, the social worker, the counselor, the special education teacher, the school psychologist, the school nurse, and the school principal (Anderson and Cardoza 2016). All of these resources come into play relative to resolving social issues in schools. Extended specialists' services, instructional time, and additional financial support for research on these issues are required.

Needed Thinking toward Helping to Resolve Social Issues Facing Public School Education

Attempts to reimagine the future of social issues in public schools and their "resolution" are troublesome at best. Easy resolutions for homelessness, poverty, mental health, juvenile services, and others escape the wisdom of even the best social science authorities. Melissa Bird (2016) reported on a visitation that she had with Richard Barth, an authority on social work and social welfare, relative to the future of social work practice in relation to what was termed "The Grand Challenge Initiative." Barth made the following futuristic recommendations: (1) We have a grand challenge on ending homelessness. Solutions might be vested in our gaining more information about their causes and using the information to see what are the opportunities and additional interventions that have compelling results. A broader range of support for child welfare, mental health services, education, and juvenile services is needed; (2) collaborative work togetherness to tackle the toughest social problems such as decarceration whereby modified family courts rule favorably for focusing on behavioral health problems; and (3) ensuring healthy youth by increasing attention to smoking prevention and changing family violence.

Launching Grand Challenges for Social Work: Toward Pinpointing the Issues

In an attempt to indicate some progress on the Grand Challenge project, the Grand Challenge networks have worked on the development of specific policy action statements. Although a set of social problem solutions would have been far more impressive, the first set of action policies were set forth in an article by ACOSA in 2018. We cite these seven specific policy action statements, since they do have major implications for projecting the issue challenges for public school education in America. Citation credit is given to Ray Boshara who was a leader in developing the focus on policy.

Policy Action Plans

1. "Ensure healthy development for all youth." Actions target family-focused interventions to children and families through primary health care.
2. "Stop family violence." Actions target improvements in the use of data to protect children and support families.
3. "Advance long and productive lives." Actions target expansion of paid family and medical leave.
4. "Create social responses to a changing environment." Actions urge development of policies targeting environmentally induced displacements in the United States.
5. "Promote smart decarceration." Actions target reversal of civic and legal exclusions for people with criminal charges and convictions.
6. "Build financial capacity and assets for all" and "Reduce extreme economic inequality." Actions target universal and progressive Child Development Accounts as a policy vehicle for lifelong asset building.
7. "Reduce extreme economic inequality." Actions target converting the Child Tax Credit into a universal child allowance. (ACOSA 2018)

This listing of guiding policy is beneficial for guiding public school activities in the area of social issues and their effects on public school programming.

But, once again, the guiding policies focus on what is needed rather than recommendations/procedures for resolving them. Give special note to the foregoing entries related to primary health care, family violence, changing environment, building financial capacity, reducing economic inequality, and lifelong asset building, topics that are discussed in this chapter specifically.

What about an Educational Tax for Everyone in the Nation?

Inequality in education financial support rises to the top of most public school concerns. We contend that every citizen in America benefits by having an educated citizenry. What about an education tax for everyone in the nation? If this would happen, we most likely would hear, "Why me? I don't even have a child in school. Isn't a free and public education a citizen's right?" The states have implemented various systems of taxation for the support of education, but none have been implemented with success over long periods of time. Even if equity could be achieved for public educational funding in some states, inequities among the fifty states would continue to be troublesome. Describing the many financial support systems implemented among the states is beyond the scope of this chapter. However, it is clear that if some revolutionary change is not instituted, financial support for education will not be resolved and financial support will remain as an inhibitor of world-class education programs in America's public schools.

Can Funding Equity for Education Ever Be Resolved?

Educational equity might need much more than just thinking outside the box. The RedforEd thrust by teachers in one state, discussed previously in chapter 2, was "resolved" temporarily when the governor of the state agreed to a plan to increase teachers' salaries by 20 percent within three years and promised enough funds to give teachers across the board an average raise of 10 percent.

The result of raises given to teachers as reported by the public school districts and charter schools ranged from 19 percent to a low of 3 percent for many school districts. "One School reported a raise of just over 1 percent" (Ruelas and Cano 2018, 1A). Regardless of the fact that practically all teachers in the state received salary increases, the salary figures differed significantly. The actual applications of the "proposed" teacher salary increases were defined and implemented in a wide variety of ways. School districts were asked to report to the Department of Education the increase in average teacher salaries from last year. The reported results were ridiculous but perhaps met the "proverbial out of the box" requirement.

For example, according to Ruelas and Cano (2018, 10A), two schools listed their average of more than 4 million percent, because the schools were new and weren't operating the previous school year. (Note: This figuring must be part of the schools' new math program.) And, in other cases, some schools appear to report their entire teacher payroll as the "average salary for all teachers." We hesitate to attempt to report the problems and mishandling of one state's so-called teacher pay plan. Their pay plan called for giving the school districts across the state an average raise of 10 percent. As noted by the news reporter's article, there is no such thing as an average school district or charter school. The accountability of all too many schools is questionable; charter school supervision commonly is missing from state requirements.

Is Public School Programming Really in the Best Interest of Every Child?

Most every publication relative to the work of public education states the principle that education should be individualized to meet the special interests and needs of all students. To what extent is such a principle actually being carried out in America's public schools today?

For example, algebra, chemistry, industrial arts, biology, and other academic subjects are basic requirements for all students in most secondary schools. Calculus is required increasingly for entrance into college and university programs. One could argue that such challenges do separate or identify talented persons, but the principle of meeting the special interests and needs of students is not revealed in mandating certain courses for high school graduation or enrolling in higher education.

One student commented that he took calculus, chemistry, biology, and industrial arts in high school but had a real interest in law. The argument that taking the aforementioned courses do something for an individual's thinking power is questionable. In regard to a career in law, an emphasis on civics, communication, logic, business law, debate, social sciences, and governance would appear to be more logical. The intent is not to disparage the courses of calculus, chemistry, and other such academic course in secondary school programs, but should these courses be required for all students?

Special summer programs related to the medical field and education were discussed earlier in the chapter. An extension of such on-site experiences in various vocational fields is recommended. In the area of industrial arts, for example, there are innumerable sites for a group of students to "experience" the real nature of the interest area that they have in mind. Such experiences are not one-day field trips; rather, they are one week or more of participation in the area at hand. School teachers in the area of experience work cooperatively with the local vocational areas in the scheduling, activity, and supervision of the on-site experience. Doing rather than observing is the key to a viable learning experience for many students. Student learning styles do differ.

Such experiences could be implemented whereby one student is involved or a small group of students participate depending on the case at hand. In one actual case, Taylor, a high school senior, spent a few weeks working with a prominent law firm. As a result of his good work, the law firm paid him to do certain law services for them. Taylor graduated from high school and continued to work with the law firm after entering college. He graduated from the university's honors college and was approved for enrollment in the law college. The law firm for which he was working offered him a position with the firm upon his completion of law school.

Yes, Taylor's experience is just one example of what can be done. However, an extension of such educational experiences is possible and can serve to get a true perspective of the students' real interest in other vocational areas. In addition, the student's learning experiences relative to cooperation, communication, relationships, governance, and other subjects of educational importance are gains made for any future pursuit.

The National Education Goals

National goals for education have been drawn and redrawn several times historically by special committees and associations. An Education Summit was held under President H. W. Bush's administration. The summit set forth eight major goals for education to be achieved by the year 2000. The goals were to serve as a nationwide pact by which the output of education systems throughout America could be measured.

In regard to the fulfillment of the stated national goals for education, Dorothy Svgdik (2010) completed an excellent study report of the Memphis public schools relative to how that school district succeeded with each of the eight national goals plus one additional goal that was added to the study goals by Memphis. The complete report analysis of goal "accomplishments" in Memphis is beyond the scope of this chapter. Nevertheless, Svgdik's report is especially well done and is illustrative of the implementation results nationally (see chapter references for information).

As one example of the Goals 2000 results, it was noted in the Svgdik follow-up study that the graduation rate in Memphis schools was 65 percent following the school district's implementation of the several 2000 goals. Goals 2000 had called for a graduation rate of at least 90 percent by the year 2000. In the following section, five of the eight 2000 goals are reviewed in regard to the most present results nationally. We keep in mind that the 2000 education goals were established several years ago in 1994. The five selected goals that are considered in the next section, however, remain relevant for education nationally.

The Status of Selected Education Goals That Remain Important for Contemporary Public Schools

Consider the following selection from the eight stated goals and how they have influenced public school education since the act was adopted in 1994.

Goal 2: *The high school graduation rate will increase to at least 90 percent.* In the recent report of the National Center for Educational Statistics (2018), the adjusted cohort rate for public high school students was 84 percent, the highest it has been since the rate was first measured in 2010–2011. In other words, more than four out of five students graduated with a regular high school diploma within four years of starting the ninth grade. This report reveals considerable progress toward the early intended goal of Goals 2000 of a 90 percent graduation rate.

Goal 5: *U.S. students will be first in the world in science and mathematics achievement.* It is quite difficult to gain specific information relative to students' academic achievement academically even though presentations on the subject are more than numerous. Procedures for collecting such data, the populations included in the data collection, the methods utilized for reporting the study data, and when the data were collected tend to result in varying study results. It is true, however, that most every study finds that U.S. students are lagging in academic subjects and certainly are not first in the world in science and mathematics achievement.

The Programme for International Student Assessment (PISA) reported that the U.S. students' academic achievement still lags that of their peers in many other countries (2017). The most recent PISA results from 2015 placed the United States at an unimpressive thirty-eighth out of seventy-one countries in mathematics and twenty-fourth in science.

Goal 6: *Every adult American will be literate and will possess the knowledge and skills necessary to compete in a global economy and exercise rights and responsibilities of citizenship.* Before attempting to assess the nation's capability to address the requirements of Goal 6, a brief explanation of national citizenship is necessary.

Authorities commonly contend that qualities needed by citizens to fulfill Goal 6, beyond the skills of reading and writing, transferable skills such as problem solving, leadership skills, and vocational skills, will be needed as well. Other skills of great importance include critical thinking, problem solving, and relevant content knowledge like environmental and climate change education, disaster risk reduction and preparedness, sustainable consumption and lifestyle; and others such as a *green economy* loom important. A green economy is one that aims at reducing environmental risks and ecological scarcities and aims for suitable development without degrading the environment.

Goal 7: *Every school in the United States will be free of drugs, violence, and the unauthorized presence of firearms and alcohol and will offer a disciplined environment conducive to learning.* An examination of the problems in public schools today make the Goal 7 seem more like a fairy tale. In an article by Boyles (2010), a survey revealed an increase of gang activity and drug use in the nation's schools. In addition, about one in four surveyed teens attending public schools reported the presence of both gangs and drugs at their schools, and 32 percent of the twelve- to thirteen-year-old middle school students said drugs were used, kept, or sold on school grounds—a 39 percent increase in just one year.

The foregoing findings suggest that as many as 5.7 million public school children in the United States attend schools with both drugs and gangs. According to Boyles' (2010) report, Califano, the director of the National Center for Addiction and Substance Abuse, says that gangs have spread far beyond the traditional urban settings and are now found in much smaller cities where they have not been recognized before.

Goal 8: *Every school will promote partnerships that will increase parental involvement and participation in promoting the social, emotional, and academic growth of children.* Finding viable information concerning the status of Goal 8 was found to be difficult. In fact, the lack of parental involvement in matters of education has been reported in most every survey of issues and problems facing teachers. However, there is a volume of literature that supports parental involvement in their child's education accompanied by long lists of positive outcomes. Just how the long lists of outcomes were scientifically determined is not always clear.

The factor(s) missing from parental involvement reports is stated in Washington's doctoral dissertation. That is, just how parental involvement impacts on students at different levels and specifically how parental involvement effects the school's Adequate Yearly Progress results are missing from school reports (2011). Washington contends that a clear understanding of activities that are impacting student achievement looms important for determining how and if parental involvement is having an effect on achievement. Washington's work did find that parents are becoming more involved in their child's education and that the old adage of communication being important is indeed being done. What is missing, as we have discussed previously, are on-site research studies on program activities that reveal specific achievement results. Surveys that report opinions and attitudes alone are insufficient.

What Does Student Health Have to Do with It?

The issue of physical and mental health disabilities has been discussed previously in the chapter. In the following section, students' general health and its influence on learning are discussed. But what does the school have to do with taking care of the health of its students? The answer is, most everything. A "sick" child will be a troubled learner. Both physical and mental disabilities influence the learning results of certain students. First of all, disabilities must be identified. Although this necessity has improved over the years, specific disabilities are still likely to be overlooked in all too many cases. Recall the case of Thelma discussed previously in this chapter. She went through grades K–12 not knowing that she suffered from dyslexia. This problem inhibited her ability to gain the advantages of a favorable elementary and secondary school education. Thelma's disability was discovered only later in her adulthood.

The physical and mental health of students is of such major importance that we recommend the extension of student health service centers on the facilities of large populated schools and appropriately located within the school-community for serving several schools within the school district. Most everyone has seen the excellent athletic facilities now available at most senior high schools. The gymnasium, track, football, basketball, track, soccer, and tennis facilities are indeed extraordinary. We visualize health facilities for school students comparable to those established for sports' activities.

The physical and mental health facilities are to service students in a variety of ways. In most cases, school specialists have their offices in the health and safety school facilities. Specialists who serve within the physical and mental health facility include a variety of specialists: medical doctors, nurses, clinical psychologists, school psychologists, educational psychologists, occupational therapists, student counselors, speech and language therapists, special learning disorders specialists, psychiatrists, truant officers, social workers, and other specialists as fits the case are available to school students within the school-community. Out of the proverbial box, you say. Not quite yet, perhaps. We also would visualize vision, hearing, and dentist professionals. And, perhaps, we could attract highly qualified educational personnel to the school district by adding free medical services administrators, teachers, and support personnel. Or, we could just remodel the school district's sports facilities and add more athletic coaches.

Improving and Building upon Our Current Federal Laws

The effort herein is not simply to comment negatively on present to improve efforts to serve students with disabilities and special needs. Rather, we do believe that America's priorities relative to other far less important activities are misplaced. It is a fact that unless education is moved up much higher on the priority list of the American people and the representatives in our governmental offices, that education will remain on the lower rungs of the priority ladder and education as the best of all worlds will remain as wishful.

In some states and in some school districts, advancements in special services for all students are evident. Since many of the special services are costly, unfortunately the majority of school districts in America do not have sufficient financial support to have them available in their support services programs. Nevertheless, the importance of special services is such that every school district in America should initiate and fully support them. Previously in this chapter, several of the special services were noted. The focus in these cases should be on assessing the outcomes of these program services and extending those that are making a positive difference for students. In other cases, the initiation of one or more of the following services might be a positive possibility.

Common special services provided in most school districts include student guidance services whereby students receive guidance related to occupational information and personal counseling relative to resolving personal problems that are being encountered by the student. Other common services include special education programs, gifted student programs, remedial education services, special social services, school psychological services, school lunch provisions, and special programs for English language learners.

An extension of student services is found in the programs of effective schools that emphasize the special needs and interests of all students. One such support service is that of programs that provide opportunities for both adults and children of low-income families to improve through programs of adult education, improved literacy education, and effective parenting relationships. Such positive activities emphasize early intervention activities that identify at an early stage those children that are not progressing well and need special attention toward becoming an effective learner. Such services are also available to homeless families and the children therein.

What about "Out of the Prison" Thinking?

Decarceration is a relative new term that centers on avoiding incarceration of students who have committed serious crimes. In brief, the program avoids placing violators of the law in prison; rather the violator is placed in a supervised program of support for helping him or her get on a positive track for positive participation in education and community life. Rather than allowing the human being to waste away in prison, every effort is made to focus on the individual's interests and special talents and rehabilitate him or her into a positive life as an American citizen. Such programs not only are advocated for children and youth but also for adult "criminals" as well.

Drucker (2016) notes that the United States puts more people into prison than any other country in the world. He contends that it is time to offer effective rehabilitation based on high-quality mental health services. Rather than having prisons, Drucker supports the establishment of social institutions to replace our prisons—social institutions that focus on healing and reconciliation. A controversial contention indeed but one that sounds more American than "living" in the negative environment of punishment institutions.

The Failing Academic Program of the Nation's Public Schools

When it comes to the major criticisms of the nation's public schools, the academic status of students in the "important" subjects of mathematics, science, and reading most often is in contention. As was noted in chapter 1, although major differences in opinions do exist, these academic subjects receive the major attention of the nation.

Results of achievement on standardized tests commonly reveal a low standing of U.S. students. Desilver (2017) noted that U.S. students continue to rank around the middle of the pack and behind many other advanced industrial nations. Wilde (2015) pointed out that on the average sixteen other industrial countries scored above the United States in science, and twenty-three scored above the United States in mathematics. Chappell (2013) commented on the test results from sixty-five countries garnered by the PISA. These earlier test results showed that American's fifteen-year-old students failed to be in the global top twenty for proficiency in reading, mathematics, and science.

A Look at Elementary School Teacher Preparation Programs

Traditionally, elementary school teachers in self-contained classrooms teach reading, arithmetic, writing, spelling, social studies, science, and sometimes both art and music. In contemporary teacher preparation programs, mathematics is one three-semester hour course as is several of the other subject-matter courses. In some school districts, specialists in music and art come into the classroom to teach music or art once each week or so.

Although the elementary school teacher is generally able to show the steps for adding, subtracting, dividing, and multiplying numbers, a basic understanding of number systems and their relationship to one another is missing from the teacher's program preparation. This fact is the primary reason that the emphasis on "new math" failed in the early 1960s. The concept of understanding rather than mechanical procedural applications in math was the new math program's intent. Understanding required additional knowledge and skill that most elementary and middle school teachers did not possess.

What the heck, let's just use a calculator! One can get the answer in five seconds, but then spend the rest of elementary and high school with little or no understanding of a number system. There is the decimal system using the number 10. For the number 345, there are 5 ones, 4 tens, and 3 hundreds. Computers today use the binary system with the base of 2. The electronic computer system can register the digits 0 and 1 in seconds. The quinary system uses a base of 5. Basic understanding of arithmetic in the elementary level lends to a higher level of understanding of more advanced mathematics in the secondary school grades. Mechanical procedures fall short in higher math courses.

Academic achievement will not approved without the opportunity to learn from subject-matter specialists. So, what's the answer? Academically, the answer centers on preparing subject-matter teachers to teach academic subjects in the early grades. It means more financial support for elementary education. It means that not just anyone who can add and subtract numbers can teach math effectively at the elementary school level.

So, why is it that so many innovations in public school programs are short-lived and tend to fade away? As was the case with the innovation of the new math, the teaching staff were not prepared to perform what the new program required. No one-week in-service program would have done the required job. A completely new approach to the program of teacher education is required. Similar preparation needs loom important for teaching science, reading, social science, and other elementary school subjects. It is true that we really do not need more information as to what is needed to improve academic performance, but we do need much more valid and reliable information about how to do it.

Another reason for the existence of "in and out" program failures is the constant interventions of the state and federal governments into local school program activities. As local school administrators have reported, a federal or state mandate is set forth that requires changes in what and how we program student instructional activities. Within a short period of time, another mandated change comes across the board that sets the first mandate aside and requires a whole new set of administrative and classroom procedures.

These changes have to be attempted or the needed financial support is not appropriated.

Comparisons with Top-of-the-List Finland

Academic comparisons of student academic achievement scores among nations commonly list Finland at or near the top of the list. What are the attributes of Finland's public education system that serve to place it above those of other countries, including the United States? Wilde (2015) set forth fourteen attributes of the Finnish education system that are viewed as contributory to the success of Finnish students. The point here is this. Finnish students do well academically and some of their educational attributes are as follows:

- The Finnish school system uses the same curriculum for all students (which may be one reason why Finnish scores varied so little from school to school).
- Students have light homework loads.
- Finnish schools do not have classes for gifted students.
- Finland uses very little standardized testing.
- Children do not start school until age seven.
- Finland has a comprehensive preschool program that emphasizes self-reflection and socializing, not academics.
- Grades are not given until high school and even then the rankings are not compiled.
- Teachers must have master's degrees.
- Becoming a teacher in Finland is highly competitive. Just 10 percent of Finnish college graduates are accepted into the teacher training program; as a result, teaching is a high-status profession. (Teacher salaries are similar to teacher salaries in the United States, however.)
- Students are separated into academic and vocational tracks during the last three years of high school. About 50 percent go into each track.
- Diagnostic testing of students is used early and frequently. If a student is in need of extra help, extensive intervention is provided.
- Groups of teachers visit each other's classes to observe their colleagues at work. Teachers also get one afternoon per week for professional development.
- School funding is higher for the middle school years, the years when children are most in danger of dropping out.
- College is free in Finland.

Several of the attributes were starred, since they appear to be unique and somewhat different from practices in U.S. schools. Wilde (2015) noted other program provisions that contribute to Finland's education success. For example, special efforts are made to focus instruction on the specific needs of different learners in terms of their skills and interests. The key here is that Finland gives special student needs a priority. Preschools are nonacademic and socialization into school culture and learning to work together with children is the primary goal.

Although preschool in Finland is not mandatory, reportedly close to 100 percent of Finland's children do attend. Comparing countries' student standardized test scores is always somewhat problematic. For example, which students are being tested (e.g., vocational versus college-bound students)? What is the nature of the nation's population? What languages are used in the homes of students? What educational funding programs and other differences weigh upon educational outcomes?

What might be learned by considering several of Finland's education attributes? For example, might provisions such as the following have implications for educational practices in the United States: the facts that all teachers must have master's degrees, the selection of teachers is based on high-quality performance record, teaching is a highly respected profession, students in high school are tracked into vocational or academic tracks, and differences of school funding have positive effects for student learning that might be integrated into public schools in the United States? Certainly, the fact that teachers are highly prized in Finland is a fact of primary importance. What other entries in Finland's listing might you attempt to implement into school practices in the United States?

Old Wine in New Bottles: Pilot Programs

Pilot programs, programs that are planned, implemented, and assessed in one school or program, are not new to education in America. Pilot programs give the school administration and teacher personnel an opportunity to implement an intervention that is closely supervised, evaluated, and assessed for possible extension within the entire school district. If the intervention is not meeting its intended purposes, it is discontinued without any major "damage" to student learning. A school district research unit would be a major component in the monitoring and assessing of such pilot interventions.

Galston (2014) supported the foregoing contention regarding piloting in stating that, "If we knew what worked, it would be so easy to fix, but because we don't know what works, that's why we have to have competition. Those who discover what works can then spread the gospel to others. . . . Take an experimental attitude. Those who discover what works can then spread the gospel to others, and we'll see, as a result, improvements across the board, up and down the line" (3).

This chapter has centered on the strong belief that both social and academic dimensions of education loom important as public school purposes. The status of the health and safety of children and youth is in direct correlation with their academic achievement. Although public schools have made great strikes in their efforts to deal with the various social issues encountered by their students, we contend that additional specialists and resources are needed to continue such improvement. Public schools in our country welcome students with a wide variety of health problems. We have underscored the need for establishing new facilities and added services to continue to meet these student needs. In chapter 4, the discussion continues to focus on the redefining of the public schools' extensions for dealing with the real educational needs of children and youth.

Key Chapter Ideas and Recommendations

- Contemporary problems and issues being encountered by the nation's citizenry are now found weighing heavily on the learning ability of children and youth in our public schools.
- The variety of student disabilities presently found in the nation's public schools necessitates an increased attention to public schools' need for special personnel and related additional resources.
- Nearly one-fourth of the children living in America show signs or symptoms of mental health problems.
- More information as to what is needed to improve the academic performance of students is not what is needed now. What is needed is more valid and effective research regarding how to improve it.
- In and out state and federal interventions have inhibited the local school's ability to focus on the specific local concerns for program improvement.
- Well-programmed and supervised pilot program interventions have the positive potential of demonstrating "what works" in the local school program.
- Stated education goals are only goals unless accompanied by the required funding support and needed changes in the preparation programs of educational personnel.
- An extension of student services is found in programs of effective schools that actually emphasize the special needs and interests of all students.
- Teacher preparation programs must be reimagined toward the goal of increasing the subject-matter knowledge and skills of elementary school teachers.
- Only 40 percent of students with emotional, behavioral, and mental problems graduate from high school.

- Authorities commonly agree that a broader range of support of child welfare, mental health sciences, and juvenile services is needed for students in grades K–12.
- Solutions to the social problems facing children and youth will require approval of a number of new policies accompanied by the allocation of personnel changes and resource allocations that are the sine qua non of their actual accomplishment.
- The purposes of education in America require the full support of the entire citizenry. All citizens, as well as America's constitutional purposes, benefit by having an educated citizenry. As stated by Thomas Jefferson, "If a nation expects to be ignorant and free, in a state of civilization, it expects what never was and never will be."

Discussion Questions

1. Assume that you are speaking at a local school meeting consisting of school staff and parents. Your topic is "School Purposes." As you open the floor for questions, one parent stands and asks, "I have kids in school and have no problem paying school taxes. However, my parents do not have kids in school anymore. Why are they still having to pay school taxes?" Write out your brief response to the parent.

2. You are a teacher at Wymore Middle School. Your friendly neighbor asks you why the school is spending so much money for services for the health and welfare of kids in school. The neighbor comments, "Isn't health and welfare a matter for the medical profession?" Write out your brief response.

3. Give thought to your local school district or a school for which you are somewhat familiar. To what extent do you believe the school is conscious of the health and security of students in the school district? What evidence or information have you been given that gives you a good picture of the school district's program for handling the social issues that it encounters?

4. School dropouts, student behavior, and academic performance have become major problems in a school in which your child is enrolled. As a parent, you have been appointed to the school's site-based council. At the first meeting of the council, the school principal has asked each council member to suggest discussion matters. How might you present your concerns relative to the foregoing problems listed above? Rather than asking what the school is

doing about dropouts, student behavior, academic performance, and others, what suggestions might you have for the council to act upon?

5. Klein set for a major change in the way teachers are compensated. For example, his proposal would compensate new teachers at much higher rates in order to attract and retain them in education. Reread the brief section in this chapter regarding Klein's recommendations. What thoughts might you have on his contentions regarding compensation. What do you think the reaction of the teachers' union/association might be regarding Klein's "out of the box" thinking?

**Case Study
We Did What Our Proposal Set Forth,
What Else Do They Expect?**

The Wymore school board established a special budget for school proposals related to the social issues and problems facing schools within the district. The door was left open for the individual school to decide on what social issue or problem might be addressed. After two meetings of the Whittier High School faculty, it was decided that the school would draft a proposal on student relations with a specific focus on student behavior including bullying and student violence. A brief proposal that included the purposes of the project and explanation of teacher and student involvement was prepared and sent to the school board for consideration. Whittier High School received a positive response regarding its proposal, which was to be initiated at the outset of the school year and completed during the last month of the school year. The $5,000 grant was to be divided as follows: The school's faculty association was to receive $2,000, the student council would receive $2,000, and $1,000 was to be made available for related project expenses.

Whittier High School planned and implemented an in-service program for teachers that included a three-week session on cooperative student/teacher relations. Special student groups met with community "experts" on the topics of student decorum, bullying's negative outcomes, and the student's responsibility for establishing a positive image of Whittier High School. Various consultants from the local community college, police department, and businesses served in the small group discussions. The high school student council drafted and approved a new "behavior" standard that all students in the school were to follow.

Near the close of the school year, the school principal drafted a project report and sent it to the school board president. The report included the following information: (1) 100 percent of the Wymore High School teachers attended the in-service session related to cooperative student/teacher relations; 76 percent of the Whittier High School student body attended at least one session on student decorum and related behavior topics. (2) In the case of the school teachers and the in-service program, 91 percent rated the program to be of "special value." (3) The members of the student council rated their communication with various community persons as being "especially interesting and enjoyable."

Each school that had an approved project received a report from the school board. Principal Reed sat at his desk with assistant principal Valentiner and examined the feedback from the school board.

"The board seems to be somewhat dissatisfied with our project results," said principal Reed. "In short, they wanted more specific hard data feedback. We told them exactly what all of us did," he said.

"Hard data," stated the assistant principal. "What could have said more specifically than we did?" he said.

Case Study Discussion Questions

1. Assume the role of principal Reed and respond to the question asked by assistant principal Valentiner.
2. Set forth at least three ways in which hard data results could have been part of the school's project proposal objectives.
3. How might a school pilot program meet the purpose of the school board's proposal request? Give one or two examples.

REFERENCES

Anderson, M., and Cardoza, K. (2016). "Mental Health in Schools: A Hidden Crisis Affecting Millions of Students," *The Mental Health Crisis in Our Schools*, part 1, *NPR ED*, August 31. https://www.npr.org/sections/ed/2016/08/31/464727159/mental-health-in-schools-a-hidden-crisis-affecting-millions-of-students.

Bird, M. (2016). "Innovating Social Work Practice for the Future." *SWHELPER*, January 29. https://www.socialworkhelper.com/2016/01/29/innovating-social-work-practice-future/.

Boyles, S. (2010). "Drugs, Gangs, on the Rise in Schools: Survey Shows Increase in Gang Activity and Drug Use in Nation's Schools." *WebMD*, August 20. https://www.webmd.com/parenting/news/20100820/drugs-and-gangs-on-the-rise-in-schools#1.

Castle, L., and Juarez, S. (2018). "Parents, Teachers Still Struggle to Buy Supplies." *Arizona Republic*, August 1, 1A.

Chappell, B. (2013). "U.S. Students Slide in Global Ranking on Math, Reading, Science." NPR, December 3. https://www.npr.org/sections/thetwo-way/2013/12/03/248329823/u-s-high-school-students-slide-in-math-reading-science.

Desilver, D. (2017). "U.S. Students' Academic Achievement Still Lags That of Their Peers in Many Other Countries." *Pew Research Center*, February 15, http://www.pewresearch.org/author/ddesilver/.

Drucker, E. (2016). "Prison is Not the Answer to Drug Abuse: Topic of Talk at UMAS." *COPH News*, Fay W. Boozman College of Public Health website, January 27. https://publichealth.uams.edu/2016/01/27/prison-is-not-the-answer-to-drug-abuse-topic-of-talk-at-uams/.

Galston, W. (2014). "Is There a Crisis?" *Frontline*, February 16. http://www.pbs.org/wgbh/pages/frontline/shows/vouchers/howbad/crisis.html.

National Center for Educational Statistics (2018, May 1). Goals that remain important for contemporary schools. *Racial Equity in Degree Attainment and State Attainment Goals*. Ed Trust, Crystal City, VA. From the web: http: //appsl.seiservicesl.com/nces/ipeds2018/Materials/the%20Education%Trust_Slide%20View_v1.pdf.

Norton, M. S., Kelly, L. K., and Battle, A.R. (2012). *The Principal as a Student Advocate: A Guide for Doing What's Best for All Students*. Larchmont, NY: Eye on Education, Inc.

Pew Research Center (2015). "U.S. Students' Academic Achievement Still Lags That of Their Peers in Many Other Countries." January 29. http://www.pewresearch.org/fact-tank/2017/02/15/u-s-students-internationally-math-science/stem_pisa/.

Ruelas, R., and Cano, R. (2018). "Report on Arizona Teachers' Salaries." *The Phoenix Republic*, August 4, 1A.

Svgdik, D. (2010). *Ed. 2000: The Race to Fix Education by the Millennium*. 2010 Rhodes Institute for Regional Studies. Memphis, TN: Rhodes College.

U.S. Department of Education (2015). "U.S. High School Graduation Rate Hits New Record High." *Achievement Gap Continues to Narrow for Underserved Students*. Washington, DC: Press Office.

Washington, A. (2011). "A National Study of Parental Involvement: Its Trends, Status, and Effects on School Success." Dissertation (477). Western Michigan University. http://scholarworks.Wonich.edu/dissertations/477.

Wilde, M. (2015). "Global Grade: How Do U.S. Students Compare?" *GreatSchools.org*, April 2. https://www.greatschools.org/gk/author/marianwilde/.

Chapter 4

Public School Education as the Best of All Worlds

Primary chapter goal: To set forth reimaginary ideas relative to public school education programs and practices that lead toward the positive goal of making public school education the best of all worlds and to support the continuation of public schools' many contributions to the nation, as well as taking revolutionary steps to remedy contemporary criticisms.

IMPROVING AND EXPANDING PROGRAM PRACTICES THAT HAVE MERIT

In chapters 1, 2, and 3, various programs and practices that have had positive influences on public education in America were noted. The extent to which these factors have been shared with schools nationally is not readily known. If education had an effective research program in place, the matter of "what works" could be shared more directly with schools throughout the nation.

In this chapter, the ways in which public schools are doing well are reemphasized. In addition, public schools' issues and problems are reviewed and followed by examples of best practices that some schools have implemented or have been recommended. Such successes should be considered by all schools that face the education difficulties being addressed. However, our reimagination purposes require that we understand the issues and problems facing education presently. We look toward major innovations that extend into the future and serve to help resolve the many problems being encountered in education today.

1. Positive Contribution of Education for Opening the Doors of Opportunity

In chapter 1, five major contributions of public school education were outlined. The first contribution underscored the concept of opening the door to a wide variety of opportunities that otherwise would not be available to each and every citizen. Education is the essential factor that gives each citizen an opportunity to succeed.

As Corso (2018) has stated, "It is inarguable that to be fully functioning members of any society children must be properly educated, a process that is thousands of years old because it is indisputably vital to the community interest" (1–2). This is the crux of the public school's major contributions to each individual and ultimately to society. As Corso points out, "Public education has always been about the development of each child as an individual to the fullest extent of their abilities." The accomplishment of this goal, in return, serves as an essential benefit to society. Thus, public education is about human development and its importance for the sustaining of quality community life, American democracy, and human civility.

The statement, "Education isn't everything, it is the only thing," is attributed to the great football coach, Vince Lombardi. Many other well-known authorities have underscored the belief that an educated populace is the answer to the challenges that face the citizenry of an ever-changing society. National presidents and others have pointed out clearly that education is vital for understanding how democracy works. Unfortunately, the subject of civics is often left off the school's course curriculum and thus more and more schools are failing to emphasize the importance of this vital subject. It opens the doors to opportunity but it also opens minds to ways of thinking crucial to our collective future.

Wexler (2018) comments, "As the nation approaches its 242nd birthday, there are signs our schools are failing to equip citizens to play the vital role the founders anticipated. For democracy to continue working, teachers need to ensure that students understand and can write analytically about the key factual information starting in elementary school" (1).

Unfortunately, education programs seem to have reduced the foregoing efforts relative to helping students understand and appreciate the underlying importance of their personal education. According to Shapiro and Brown (2018), "Civic knowledge and public engagement is [sic] at an all-time low. . . . Without an understanding of the structure of government; rights and responsibilities; and methods of public engagement, civil literacy and voter apathy will continue to plague American democracy" (1).

Being prepared to become involved in practicing and improving democratic principles and human civility looms significant for effective citizenship in America. The goal of citizenship, the allegiance to the American flag, the importance of voting, the nature of cooperation, and one's importance in fostering a positive social contract among the citizenry are among those concepts that public school education can help children and youth learn and practice in their daily lives.

These are important values that can be learned and practiced within the doors of the local public school and the learner's school-community. The crux of the matter is that unless the nation places the primary emphasis on establishing the value of civility within and among all its people, the goal of being the best of all worlds educationally is only a high hope.

The school curriculum must be expanded in order to give due attention to the importance of American democracy and how an educated citizenry is of paramount importance for sustaining its foundational principles. Freedom and responsibility are inextricably related. It is not just being able to do anything or everything that one wants to do. A civil society cannot be sustained unless each citizen is properly educated in America's effective public schools.

> As the nation approaches its 242nd birthday, there are signs our schools are failing to equip citizens to play the vital role the founders anticipated. For democracy to continue working, teachers need to ensure that students understand and can write analytically about key factual information starting in elementary school. (Wexler 2018, 1)

It is beyond the scope of this chapter to set forth a comprehensive K–12 topic list for instruction in civics. However, basic knowledge for lessons in the middle school grades should be reconstituted to bring back the importance of citizenship for sustaining the basic values and principles of American democracy. Although not new to many school programs historically, a reemphasis of civics seems necessary in contemporary school programs.

1. *The U.S. Constitution and the Bill of Rights.* The guiding document for America's democracy and the rights guaranteed for all citizens and respective responsibilities that accompany such rights loom important. Citizenship as defined in such documents as the Declaration of Independence, Bill of Rights, Articles of Confederation, and the U.S. Constitution provides guidance for citizen involvement in their school-community.

2. *The checks and balances of governmental authority as demonstrated through the legislative, executive, and judicial branches of government.* Participative citizens must understand how the three major branches of government serve to support and balance the laws and decisions that are guided by the provisions of the U.S. Constitution. Understanding the concept of powers of a democratic government, how these powers are determined and balanced, and the role of citizenship in reserving these values is an educational purpose of major importance.

3. *Citizenship as revealed in the civil rights provisions, voting/elections, U.S. symbols (flag, Statue of Liberty, Star Spangled Banner, etc.).* The importance of loyalty and how such behavior is demonstrated by the individual citizen is of paramount importance. Each citizen must understand that the flag is not just a representation of the first thirteen colonies and the fifty states but must know how it represents the values embedded in a democracy and the sacrifices made by many to retain the freedoms that all citizenry enjoy. Gaining an understanding of how each individual can become involved in promoting the values for which the country stands serves to foster the concept of democracy.

4. *How a bill becomes law and how the people play a crucial role in making decisions relative to what and how proposed bills are approved and implemented.* The learner should gain some understanding of the process that a bill "goes through" before its final approval. The process serves to demonstrate how our democracy works and the checks and balances that keep the focus on justice.

5. *The judicial system as it is practiced at the local, state, and federal levels.* Emphasis is placed on the component of the nature of a trial by jury whereby citizens commonly rule on the outcome of the case at hand. A study of several of the important court decisions that have had major impacts on the rights of the citizenry, immigration, racism, education, freedom of speech, student rights, and others serves an important purpose relative to rights and justice in the American system.

6. *Appreciation of the nation's and states' leaders.* Appropriate attention to the contributions and sacrifices of America's leaders serves an important lesson. A study of the specific contributions that the presidents of the United States have made toward the initiation, implementation, and support of public school education in America gives students an understanding of the comprehensive responsibilities of the nation's leaders including the welfare of all citizens.

But isn't all of the foregoing information taking place in all schools today? Those in the teaching profession tell us that it is not. The time and effort of the professional staff have focused on the academic subjects of mathematics, science, and reading. We emphasize the need for new curricular thinking whereby education is viewed as being more extensive than the important aforementioned subjects. Civics, art, music, vocational education, language, technology, and other courses that have "suffered" due to the government's emphasis on math and science necessarily must be reinstated in the schools' curriculum or the target of "best of all worlds" for education cannot be met.

2. Positive Contribution of Education for Being Inclusive in Regard to All Students

Chapter 1 set forth the major program services that public schools commonly provide all students according their special needs. The primary contributions of the federal government to education have been defined in part in the legislative bills approved during the twenty-five-year history of the Individuals with Disabilities Education Act (IDEA) of 1997. This legislation was enacted to support states and localities in protecting the rights of, meeting the individual needs of, and improving the results for all children and youth to receive special education and related services (U.S. Department of Education [USED] 2007). IDEA not only was revolutionary in its contributions to public school inclusiveness but has also continued to address needed improvements for special needs infants, children, and youth. The major successes of IDEA are noted in the following section. The importance of this legislation is demonstrated by its continuation of extending and meeting the new special student needs that inevitably occur in this program area of paramount importance.

The impressive progressive programs for educating children with disabilities cannot be completely detailed in this chapter. Nevertheless, we underscore the accomplishments of IDEA and the implementation of programs within our nation's public schools regarding the American value of inclusiveness and equality in educational opportunities. One can reimagine the continuing future program practices in this area of public school education. Reportedly, over 200,000 eligible infants, toddlers, and their families are provided special services related to special needs. Six million other special needs children continue to be serviced by the nation's public schools.

Special Needs Program Improvements Have Been Extraordinary

In the early 1960s, few public schools nationally had special education programs in operation. Give thought to the progress that public schools have achieved. Over the years, special education has grown and special services have been provided for approximately 6 million children and youth. Best total enrollment for the nation's public schools has been reported to be 50,094,000 students. With approximately 6 million special needs students being serviced, the results would indicate that approximately 12.0 percent of the nation's public school students are being helped by special service programs. The commonly reported, 20 percent, is questionable. Nevertheless, the percentage is increasing as new disabilities are discovered and the inclusion of some services for children who were previously excluded such as blind, deaf, emotionally disturbed, or mentally retarded.

Our purpose here is to applaud the accomplishments of the nation's public schools for their positive achievements in the area of special student needs and to recommend continued research and personnel competencies for identifying and ultimately providing additional services for all special needs students and at the same time underscore the fact that the excellent progress of the last twenty-five years must be continued toward the goal of earlier discovery, earlier treatment, and earlier remediation of many of the disabilities now being encountered by students.

We refer the reader back to the previous chapter discussion on the establishment of a special services unit for each school district that would place specialists in charge of specific special needs programs. In summary, the future of public school programming, relative to inclusiveness, must give serious thought and action to (1) building on its previous support for equality of access to expand and strengthen its support for quality programs and services; improving educational results for children with disabilities. Individual approaches to accessing the educational opportunities within the curriculum for each disabled child; (2) focusing teaching and learning that leads to high achievement for all; and (3) continue to underscore the principle that each citizen, including individuals with disabilities, has a right to participate and contribute in a positive way to society (USED 2007).

3. The Positive Contribution of Education for the Improvement of Teacher Preparation Programs

Criticism of the preparation programs for teachers is common in today's literature. Although preparation programs are overdue for major improvement, current preparation programs do represent major improvements that have been established over the years. Teaching in the early years of the 1840s was not an engaging career for the large majority of educated adults. Individuals entered teaching without any particular preparation for the role. Male students, particularly, were encouraged to learn to read so that they could read the Bible and perhaps enter the ministry.

Horace Mann was the first person to introduce the teacher institute for prospective and practicing teachers in order to learn something of teaching skills, mapping, and related schooling. Reportedly, Mann took it upon himself to promote teacher improvement in teacher institutes, and although he requested funding for the program, he was refused so he funded them out of his own pocket.

In the early 1800s, Mann worked to develop the common school, which ultimately established the grading system that placed children in grades according to their age. The establishment of the normal schools was a revolutionary happening in the history of American public schools. Persons who aspired for a teaching role in education were able to receive the high achievement of licensing after only two years. Ultimately, of course, the two-year normal school developed into the nation's four-year colleges whereby an individual could earn a bachelor's degree within four years. The four-year preparation program continues in universities nationally, although most single salary schedules for teachers give salary raises to teachers who earn a master's degree in some area of education.

Teacher preparation has been listed under the positive accomplishments of education since it has, without question, made significant positive improvements over the years. The requirements of having a four-year college degree, along with other education professional preparation for teachers, have indeed been greatly improved. Nevertheless, the preparation of teachers continues to be criticized and often is listed among those educational programs that must be improved. Unfortunately, professional growth requirements for teachers in all too many school districts are unsatisfactory.

For example, one school district's professional growth requirement stated that a teacher must earn an additional six semester hours of college credit within every six years. With such a requirement, a teacher could attend summer school and earn six semester hours of credit in the first year of teaching and do nothing more for the following five years. In other cases, the college credit requirements do not have to be earned in the teacher's subject area in which he or she is teaching.

Recommendations for reimagining the preparation program for teacher personnel are discussed later in the chapter. However, teacher preparation as it applies to practicing teachers is discussed in the following section. Those school districts with high-quality professional development programs center on the concept of the talent development plan (TDP). At the outset, we make note of the fact that high-quality teachers commonly "demand" opportunities for personal and professional development.

Empirical evidence shows, that if high-quality teachers are not are not provided such development activities, they will be drawn to schools districts that do have such provisions available. Because continuous professional development is such an important part of assuring the individual teacher's professional and personal growth, the following section sets forth important steps that must be continued and extended.

We contend that professional development is self-development. That is, the individual takes charge of his or her personal growth with guidance from a qualified mentor. The TDP has four distinct steps: (1) establishing the mentor-protégé relationship; (2) preparing the protégé to work on the TDP; (3) identifying the talent development areas of strength and others for development; and (4) establishing goals and objectives and the action plan to accomplish them (Norton 2008, 206). Step 1, the establishment of the mentor-protégé relationship and how they will work together to accomplish the stated goals is foremost in importance. In step 2, the purposes and procedures of the TDP are clarified and recommendations for assessing personal strengths are set forth; then in step 3, the focus is on the identified strengths of the protégé and how they can be implemented in the improvement plan. The final step 4 centers on the identification of the protégé's personal strengths and areas for further development. The mentor takes the main position of a listener and serves to direct the protégé's attention to how their strengths are or could be further advanced in present work activities.

4. The Positive Contribution of Education Relative to Sending High School Graduates to College

Reported statistics relative to high school students and readiness for college tend to differ. We do understand that the majority of literature reports criticize the lack of high school graduates' readiness for college. A close estimate of student attendance in college, however, is that approximately 35.6 percent of all high school graduates leave high school ready for college. One report of some interest stated that of all U.S. citizens of ages eighteen to twenty-four, more than 33 percent are currently in college. If, indeed, this report by the National Center for Higher Education Management Systems (NCHEMS 2015) is correct, having more than one-third of high school graduates in college in America is worthy of mention as a positive high school contribution to American society.

No, not all of these college students will achieve the bachelor of science degree but are representative of the success of the public schools in many respects. In addition, the knowledge that these persons do receive provides a stronger readiness for positions in various careers and services as citizens in our American society.

We keep in mind that many high school graduates go on to vocational schools, serve in the military, or assume other worthy career positions whereby they gain additional knowledge and skills and become highly successful business leaders. For example, Ed Sutton, a fictitious name given to a high school graduate of a small high school in a central Midwest state, started a co-ownership of a very small used car business in a small suburban town. From that beginning, he went on to serve four successful years in the military service, was discharged, and went to the west coast and initiated several small business enterprises.

His high-quality skills as a businessman and politician earned him an appointment as the officer in charge of the state's public school facilities program. Ed's knowledge and skills related to school facilities allowed him to implement a statewide business related to school facility planning. He served as president of this highly successful company for several years during which time he extended his talents into several other successful business enterprises. Ed is only one example of a high school graduate who made major contributors in various occupations that served toward the improvement of the nation's welfare.

5. The Positive Contribution of Social Mobility in Relation to Facilitating a Shared Culture and Sustaining a Democratic Society

Perhaps Corso (2018) has said it best. In his article, "The Importance of Public Education," Corso stated,

> It is inarguable that to be fully functioning responsible members of any society children must be properly educated, a process, that is thousands of years old because it is un-disputably vital to the community interest.... The foundational conception of public education is neither capitalism nor socialism, it is not Republicans nor Democrats, and it has never been, before now, about profit. Public education has always been about the development of each child as an individual to the fullest extent of their abilities for the ultimate benefit of society. Public schools are about Community, about Democracy, about Civility. The antithesis of self-centeredness is Community and Community means working together, learning and teaching, not grasping whatever we can be at whatever cost to others, oblivious to an inclusive social contract. Public education is where children learn and practice these values. (1–3)

Corso's statement emphasizes the reasons why so much attention is given to the importance of completing a public school education, understanding one's opportunities and responsibilities as a citizen, and living successfully in the shared culture of a democratic society.

Silverberg (2016) reminds us that public education not only opens the doors to opportunity but also opens the minds to critical thinking. Why is critical thinking so important? The person with the ability to think clearly has the opportunity to visualize the many open doors that are there for his or her economic well-being and enjoyment of life. Public education provides an opportunity for everyone to become acquainted with a broader picture of the need to give full attention to the learning of new knowledge and development of new skills that lead to a greater ability to think wisely about available choices and "the roads to take."

*The Inhibitors of Effective Public Education
and Thinking Outside of the Proverbial Box*

It is not our intention to assume that our "out of the proverbial box thinking" has never been mentioned by someone else somewhere at some time. In fact, as one watches the History channel on TV nowadays, perhaps some of our ideas have already appeared on the hieroglyphics by aliens who many believe visited and lived on earth many centuries ago. Or, perhaps not.

In chapter 2, six major problems or failures of public school educations were identified as being discussed in the literature and contended by the citizenry nationally. Each problem inhibits education in the United States to become the best of all worlds. These problems were as follows: (1) the lack of adequate financial support for public school education; (2) the many inequities in public school education within the states and nation; (3) the widening of the control of public school education by various government agencies and power groups; (4) the increasing lack of highly qualified teacher personnel; (5) the continuation of poor academic performance on the part of students nationally; and (6) the number of small inefficient school districts including the growing number of administrative personnel and unsatisfactory organizational development practices. We add a seventh major problem at this point that centers on the lack of a research base that supports the best educational program practices for effective teaching and student learning.

Previous chapters have included discussions of needed interventions in matters of public school education and a repetition of these needed changes are not to be included in this chapter. We do, however, add to the possibilities of extended and/or revolutionary changes in relation to the six foregoing inhibitors of public school education in America. Before doing so, however, we remind the reader of our earlier discussion of doing the impossible.

Education Inhibitor #1
The Lack of Financial Support for Public School Education

In chapter 2, the thinking of Klein regarding revolutionary changes in teacher compensation was noted. The ingenuity of Klein's financial thinking receives our immediate support. Klein's thinking contains the following major changes in the provisions and rationale for education compensation practices. It not only promotes the potential interest of high-quality individuals to consider education as a career field but also places the focus of compensation on quality teaching performance as opposed to the present system that centers on years of service regardless of the level of service provided.

Klein's plan for fixing the present compensation schemes centers on five revolutionary fixes for funding the compensation of the professional teaching staff.

1. Rather than paying for many years for longevity and lifetime benefits, the focus of the compensation plan must be on attracting, hiring, and rewarding excellence. The single salary system of today, which contains

automatic salary increases and promises of large retirement benefits much later in life, is to be eliminated. This elimination saves funds that are used for giving excellent service, rewards for serving in difficult teaching assignments, and giving school districts the ability to seek and hire highly prepared and knowledgeable teaching personnel in all shortage areas of the curriculum. In addition, the arrangements would allow for the subject-matter specialization of elementary teachers and eliminate the present practices of having the teacher attempting to be qualified to teach all subjects in his or her self-contained classroom (Klein 2011).

2. In addition, Klein's frontloading strategy of compensation is the kind of "out of the box" thinking that is needed toward ultimately resolving the inhibiting factor of inadequate financial support for education. That is, frontloading compensation, whereby new teachers could receive high salaries that would compete advantageously with other professions, was to save large amounts of money for the aforementioned educational services.

New teachers would receive as much as $80,000 within four years of teaching service. The concept theoretically would not only serve for attracting new highly qualified individuals to education but would also serve toward the resolution of retaining teachers in the educational profession. Education personnel would receive the frontloading of compensation in the early years of their career and not have to wait twenty-five or more years to receive monies from the present back-loaded compensation structure. Klein's thinking of compensating the early years of a teacher's experience would obviate the need of their waiting for the end of a long career to receive a payback. In short, Klein's thinking of eliminating the lifetime, defined pensions, amortizing savings, and then paying it to teachers in their early years represents one of those impossible proposals that could become possible.

We tend to give full support to a performance plan whereby compensation is based on high-quality performance rather than service time.

Honda and Weingarten (2015) set forth an article that centered on funding public school education in the twenty-first century. At the time of their writing, Honda represented California's seventeenth Congressional District and had served in the House since 2001. He sat on the Appropriations Committee and also had lengthy service as a teacher. Weingarten was president of the American Federation of Teachers. These writers expressed the opinion that funding for public schools is based on an antiquated and unfair system and contended that a new funding system, such as they set forth, would give all children the chance to climb the ladder of opportunity. Poverty was underscored as being a major education inhibitor. The authors were recommending a report by the U.S. Department of Education's Equity and Excellence

Commission as being a roadmap for serving to remedy the problem of poverty and student academic outcomes.

The Department of Education's model recommended investing in high-quality pre-K programs to make sure poor children and those with disabilities did not trail their peers at the very outset of school attendance. It recommended, what was termed wraparound services, pre-K programs to make certain that children from poverty families did not come to school unprepared. Health care and related social services were illustrative services. The funding plan recommended support for the necessary training of teachers as well. Since 2015, the focus on remediating inequality in education for all students has been a primary topic of conversation and concern.

Education Inhibitor #2
Inequities in the Support and Provisions for Public School Education

It is puzzling to think about inequities in public school education in view of the fact that an infant has no say whatsoever regarding the state in which he or she is born or state(s) that he or she resides in during the K–12 school years. Those decisions depend largely on the circumstances of the parents. One might be born and raised in a state highly rated in regard to its public school program and then might move to Mississippi that has one of the lowest-ranking public school systems in America. On the other hand, he or she might have been born in Mississippi and attended public school there in grades K–12. Upon graduation, the family might have moved to a high-quality education state to live for the next ten years. Why should the state in which one is born and lives determine the quality of education that is received? In a democratic society, it really should not make a significant difference in the quality of education depending on the state of residence.

The state holds the responsibility for education but due to the wide differences of property values among the states, inequities in educational support are inevitable. Equity in education will remain undoable as long as this condition exists. A required per-pupil monetary support should be established in all states in the nation. This tax rate should be determined by the amount of financial support that is needed minimally to support public school education in America. That is, what per-pupil dollar figure is needed to support education in America's public schools effectively? One strategy is to have each state assess an education tax rate on property established by the federal government. If that tax rate collects the funds required in the state to support education at the required level, no additional local or state funds are required. If not, the federal government makes up the difference needed to meet the equitable per-pupil monetary support set forth for the nation's schools.

It should be clear that some states will meet the minimum requirement with the very first annual taxation. Other states will collect tax funds that are over the minimum requirement. In that case, tax refunds are in order. If a state's taxation does not result in getting sufficient funding for the per-pupil requirement, the difference is to be allocated by the federal government. The state per-pupil standard is set so that school programs in any state have excellent support in terms of personnel and facility resources. But won't such an educational funding program increase the funding responsibilities upon the federal government? Most likely, the answer is "Yes." In the end, high education quality is related closely to what the citizenry is willing to pay for.

The foregoing education finance plan is somewhat similar to present funding practices in some states. However, amendments are attached to a state's tax plan that allows the community voters to approve large monetary overrides for education, which some states can easily afford and other states cannot. Inequity becomes an ongoing issue. In any case, suggestions to support education through foundations, reducing the number of administrative personnel, or by cutting certain extracurricular school activities have little chance of meeting the financial needs of education. Citizens want a world-class public school program and, with the same voice, want "no new taxes."

Education Inhibitor #3
The Widening Loss of Educational Control at the Local School Level

As has been pointed out previously in several sections of the book, school boards within and among the states differ greatly. At the present time, local school boards commonly receive their authority from the state legislature. However, empirical evidence makes it clear that school boards in America commonly reflect four different levels of decision making: elite or dominated, pluralistic, factional, and inert. However, under present circumstances, we might add the label of controlled. The label of controlled differs from that of elite in that elite boards are governed primarily by a community power group or individual that has a great influence on whether a particular board policy or program will or will not be implemented. Such groups are generally known whereby elite influentials work behind the scenes and are not acting at the front of community affairs.

A controlled board is one that has virtually lost its governance authority by authorizing its policy and regulation development to be done by an outside association. An elite board is greatly influenced and controlled by a small group of community influentials or one individual who has the ability to control the outcomes of such matters as school bond issues, appointments of school officials, the implementation or withholding of certain curricular programs, and so forth.

However, a large part of a school board's loss of control is the fact that its members lack the preparation and experience for assuming such responsibility. As a governance body, the school board is mainly responsible for establishing the policies that set forth the aims/purposes that the school is to accomplish. Only the school board has the authority to adopt school policy. Unless school board members can distinguish between a policy, administrative regulation, and a bylaw, the chances of having effective organization within the school district are slim if not impossible.

Reimagining the Requirements and Licensing of School Board Member

Presently, there are three requirements most common in all the states for becoming a school board member: (1) being a resident of the school district, (2) being an eligible voter, and (3) not having been convicted of a felony or being a convicted sex offender. Other requirements within some states are possessing at least a high school diploma, not being an employee of the school district, being at least twenty-one years of age, and, in a few cases, not being related to any employee in the school district. Only the requirement of having a high school diploma or GED certificate speaks in any way of needing education or experience qualifications for the position.

If public education in the United States is to reach the goal of being the best of all worlds, it seems reasonable to require a licensing program that includes subjects on the functions and responsibilities of governing boards, school policies and administrative regulations, business practices, school public relations, school board/superintendent/staff relations, school-community relations, public school purposes, school facility planning, student services, state and federal legislation, school law, the school curriculum, school board member development activities, and others as fits the case. If education in America is to reach the best of all worlds, it should be governed by the best of all persons that serve as its governing body.

The state requirements for being eligible for school board membership minimally should require the completion of the licensing class requirements set forth by the state as noted above and completion of a mock school board program sponsored by the state school board association and state education department. A three- or four-year license would be awarded to the potential school board member; the formal voting process would be in place for electing a person with a license to an official school board position.

We favor the compensation of school board members for their service. The reason to serve as a school board member commonly is stated "to give some payback to my community." This purpose can be fulfilled just as well if the person is compensated for the time and service that he or she gives to the school-community.

Education Inhibitor #4
The Inability to Hire and Retain
Highly Qualified Teacher Personnel

Previously, in this chapter, the need to increase educational funding and the changes needed for compensating school personnel were addressed. However, other major improvements in the way education views its teacher personnel are needed as well. At the secondary level, little change in the work schedule or workload of teachers has been witnessed over the years. Traditionally, the secondary school teacher teaches five classes each day five days a week. That workload adds up to be approximately twenty-five hours in the classroom each week and one hundred hours each month. The elementary teacher commonly teaches five hours a day for five days each week. Once again, this classroom time equals twenty-five hours a week or one hundred hours each month.

The actual teacher load of one individual, however, is constituted by other important factors. For example, the subject taught, the number of classes taught, the actual length of the class periods, class size, the number of class preparations, and the extracurricular assignments of the teacher make major differences in the workload of the teacher. Teacher load studies have shown clearly that teacher loads within any one school are inequitable. That is, in most any school situation, the teacher with the highest teacher load has a teacher load index as much as two times greater than the teacher with the lowest teacher load (Norton 2008). Furthermore, it is not unusual to find that the newest teachers in the school are carrying the highest load indices.

The topic of teacher load and scientific ways to measure it have been on record for many years. Teacher load is one of the problems whereby ways to equalize it among the faculty have been available but have been ignored by educational administrators and other educators. The calculation of teacher load for secondary schools was first considered by Douglass in 1951, approximately seven decades ago. A recommended teacher load formula for elementary school teachers was introduced by Norton and Bria nearly three decades ago, and it too has been ignored over the years. Education does have research on many important topics that have just slipped through the cracks of ineffective program operations. Once again, we note the crucial need for implementing a strong research base for educational practice.

A Lightbulb Experience

A school district in Nebraska instituted a scientist for teacher day once each year. Individuals in various "scientific positions" in the community were selected to take the place of the teachers in the local school system. The activity gave an opportunity on one day for teachers to take part in appropriate professional development activities while students gained the opportunity to learn about various technological and science activities in the world of work.

In one case, one junior high school in the school district invited Mr. Henson, the chief engineer for the Lincoln Telephone and Telegraph Company, to teach classes for one day on the various "scientific" activities of that company. The invitee did not teach the specific subject matter that was commonly taught in the class but rather focused on the "scientific" activities that were especially important in the telephone business. Mr. Henson and other scientists served as instructors for the full day of five class sessions.

At the close of the school day, the school principal invited Mr. Henson and other special guests to the teachers' lounge for refreshments. Mr. Henson entered the lounge and dropped down in his chair. Then he exclaimed, "My #&@, do teachers do this everyday!"

Hood (1993) citied Doyle of the Hudson Institute who wrote, "There is no mystery as to how to find and retain qualified teachers of mathematics or the sciences. Pay them what the market demands, provide them with the benefits that are competitive, and create a work environment in which they can derive genuine professional satisfaction. Pay differentials are the answer" (8). We repeat this contention once again more than twenty-five years later but doubt that education will listen.

The teacher's day from 7:30 a.m. to 4:30 p.m. or so has to be changed completely. Professional teachers should be accorded the same professional work opportunities as professionals in higher education. Scheduling and determining the number of students in any instructional situation needs controlled pilot program researching. In some instances, the most highly qualified teacher of an academic subject might have a greater class size than traditionally considered as best practice. In other situations, a teacher might work closely with a class of five, ten, or fifteen students. We do not support the contention that large-sized classes are always settings for poor learning. The size of any one class should depend more on student learning styles than the number of students in the class and the research results of student learning.

Organizational arrangements for class hours also need redefining. Might it be more productive to have a class in science, art, music, or civics for two-and-half hours twice a week allowing the teacher to be free for two-and-half hours twice a week as well? The point is that teacher time must be redefined professionally—perhaps similar to that of a university professor. The professional teacher, like the professional instructor in higher education, should have blocks of time when engagement in such activities as action research can be addressed.

Practicing school principals have gone on record indicating that they do not feel prepared to deal with the increasing responsibilities and related complex problems that they encounter today. Course work in such contemporary areas as curriculum development, student achievement improvement, learning theory, parental relations, instruction technology, data analysis, dealing with student drug violations, and others commonly are among the topics that are not effectively presented in their preparation programs.

While the workload of the school principal continues to increase and the need for improved assistant principal numbers and responsibilities is evident, one of the most often cited criticisms of education is that it is top-heavy administratively. Empirical evidence does not support this contention. In fact, the ratio of administrative staff to employees supervised is lowest of other large businesses and industrial enterprises. What is needed is a complete change of public professional responsibilities of school assistant principals so that the school principal can assume the role of the CEO of the local school enterprise. In this regard, we recommend the reader get a copy of the book, *The Assistant Principal's Guide: New Strategies for New Responsibilities* (Norton 2015).

Our thinking places the preparation of teacher personnel outside the walls of the all too many higher education facilities in operation today. A teacher/administrator academy should be established that offices the best of all world's professorial personnel who have had high levels of success at the public school level in charge of the preparation program. The school district's research units should be located in the same learning center. The aforementioned student services unit might well be attached or closely situated to the academy facility.

Three common "strategies" for preparing prospective teachers are practiced today in many university preparation programs. One procedure is that of placing aspiring teachers in public schools within the university area. If, indeed, the public schools in America are failing, why would we want to prepare our aspirant teachers at these sites under the supervision of poor-performing teachers and principals? Aspiring teachers need to be prepared in the most highly successful learning centers that the states can establish.

A Model for the Preparation of Public School Teachers

Four years ago, Rowman & Littlefield featured a book, *The Changing Landscape of School Leadership: Recalibrating the School Principalship*. One section of that book sets forth revolutionary procedures for preparing school principals. The recommended preparation model is addressed in the following section of this chapter. Schools that are representative of being the best of all worlds need to have leaders who also are the best of all worlds. This is not happening today. All too many preparation master's degree programs for school principals are completed online. Distance preparation programs are questionable. This programming is not producing the quality of administrators to overcome the inhibiting educational problems/issues being discussed in this book.

The national concern for significant improvement in the attraction, recruitment, and preparation of school leaders certainly is not a new contention. Various individuals, education boards, leadership institutes, and other education-related interest institutions historically have reported on the existing problems related to preparation programs for school principals. Two early comprehensive reports on the topic of principal preparation were completed by the Southern Regional Education Board (SREB)—one in April of 2001 and the other in 2003. Six specific strategies were recommended for improving the preparation programs for school principals.

We include SREB's six strategies herein, even though there is little evidence that these recommendations were ever given much attention since being reported nearly seven years ago. However, each strategy remains worthy of being brought to the attention of the readers: Strategy #1—Identify high performers and single them out as future leaders; Strategy #2—Recalibrate preparation programs by establishing new leadership standards that focus on results for students; Strategy #3—Emphasize real-world training. Reimagine great hands-on involvement in schools that have records of high-quality performance; Strategy #4—Link principal licensure to performance that is monitored and evaluated by school leaders that have, themselves, been licensed after highly successful training activities; Strategy #5—Move highly qualified teachers into leadership roles; and Strategy #6—Establish state administrative academies to cultivate leadership activities that focus on the best of all world's education results.

We add our recommendations for making major improvements in administrative preparation programs in the following section.

1. There is a vital need for improving the quality of candidates for the principalship by reducing and/or eliminating the number of programs that claim to be preparing school leaders. These online programs and programs that are relegated to practicing school leaders must be eliminated. They may be licensing number of individuals but are not being prepared or qualified to program high-quality administrative programs.

2. Recruitment of high-quality school leaders should begin by fostering their interest in education before entering college. Many schools have business day activities, vocational guidance programs, career interest inventories, and other activities for almost every occupation one can think of. Why not have such activities that center on leadership and opportunities in an education career?

3. Most every student in public schools knows something about their school principal. But what do they really know about his or her challenging work and the variety of knowledge and skills required in the role of school principal? How many students really know about the many specialist leadership

opportunities in school district settings? Early interests in education can be fostered in social studies classes and special civics classes.

4. Most schools have business visitation days when students select community sites to visit and learn about the knowledge and skills needed for careers in various business and industrial organizations in the school-community. Why not a visitation day that includes the ins and outs of a major school district's operations? The climax to such a day's investigation of a school district's operations might end with the students' attendance at a school board meeting.

5. We recommend a credit class in Education 101. Fifty percent of the class would include serving as a teacher or school principal assistant at a school of choice. High school students might serve such assistance roles in the elementary schools that are within the school district.

A Recommended Preparation Model

Public School Program Offerings in the Field of Education

- Importance of Education in America—Its Contribution
- The Opportunities in a Teaching Career
- What Is Educational Administration; Its Career Opportunities
- School Visitations
- Education Club Activities
- Student "Teaching" Experiences

Entering College to Earn a BS Degree in Education

- Program Specializations
- Entry Requirements:
  - Admission Testing
  - GPA and Other Test Results
  - *SAT Scores*
  - Critical Reading 680–780
  - Mathematics 690–780
  - Writing 690–780
  - *ACT Scores*
  - Composite 31–34
  - English 32–35
  - Mathematics 31–35
  - General Science 31–35
- General Studies
- Education Program Studies

- Degree Specializations
- Student Teacher Observations/Classroom Teaching

Graduate Education in State-Approved MA Administrative Program of Studies Supervised by Sanctioned State Education Institutes or Approved Universities

- Core Courses in Educational Administration:
- Curriculum and Supervision Specialty Courses (elementary, middle school, secondary school, mathematics, English, science, civics, social science, fine arts, business, and others)
- Learning Leadership
- Finance/Business Specialty
- The Student as a Learner
- Technology in the School Program
- Human Resources Administration
- School Climate and Student Achievement
- The Learning Culture in the School
- Principal/Assistant School Principals as Learning Leaders
- Student Relatives
- On-Site Program Practices
- Residency Year Experiences
- One-Year Residency and Administrative Licensing Requirements

Entering Administrator Academy for Approved PhD Administrative Program of Studies

- One-Year Specialty Program—results in the obtaining of a three-year administrative license for the positions of assistant school principal, curriculum coordinator, human resources director, and other equivalent level administrative positions.
- Two-Year Specialty Program—results in the obtaining of a five-year administrative license for the position of school principal, elementary, middle, or secondary school level.
- Three-Year Specialty Program—results in the obtaining of a five-year license for the position of assistant school superintendency. The school superintendency requires the completion of the doctoral degree in education.

Individuals who meet all enrollment requirements and are accepted to the administrative academy have all related expenses for each licensing program paid by the federal and state agencies. A doctoral dissertation is required, which must center on a research topic of special interest and need of the state in which the administrative academy is located.

Professional Development Program Requirements: Closely Supervised by the State's Administrative Academy

The foregoing preparation model is designed to meet three primary educational purposes as set forth by Norton (2015):

1. Fostering the early interest of young people in education through planned programs that underscores the important opportunities that it provides and encouraging talented young children and youth to participate in educational activities similar to what one might do relative to an early interest in nursing, law, or business enterprise;

2. Upgrading the preparation of educational leadership programs toward the goal of promoting visionary leadership attitudes accompanied by extensive knowledge and experience that focus on leadership for positive change relative to administrator preparation and continued professional development for all school leaders; and

3. Reemphasizing the paramount importance of educational support by all local, state, and federal agencies for establishing a financial support structure for education that ensures the attraction of high-quality personnel into the career field of education and educational administration.

Educational Inhibitor #5
Poor Student Academic Performance

The many criticisms of public school education seldom, if ever, leave out the problem of poor academic performance on the part of student learners. The literature is full of information relative to the poor standing of American students in the areas of mathematics, science, and reading. The solution to this problem is vested in the various solutions set forth in this chapter: increase of high-quality teacher personnel, much improved preparation of teachers at both the elementary and secondary levels of school programming, revolutionary changes in the compensation methods for beginning teacher personnel, and stronger subject-matter instruction at the elementary school level in mathematics, science, and civics.

Obviously, the directed increases in support of public school financial support, including the elimination of the many inferior preparation programs for teachers and administrators, must be planned and implemented rather than just being talked about. The preparation institutes discussed in this chapter should replace the present teacher preparation programs in "institutions" that are not qualified to meet the instructional requirements needed for personnel in quality schools. The difficulty to hire high-quality subject-matter teachers and administrative personnel can only be resolved by implementing the kinds of recommendations set forth in this chapter. Although purposely based on thinking outside the proverbial box, steps toward the accomplishment of the needed purposes will not occur with high hopes alone; program implementation must accompany them.

Education Inhibitor #6
The Disorganization of Public School Districts Relative to the Most Important Factor of Organizational Development

One thing that the public school can do that would not cost more money, although it might save some financial expenditures, is by giving much more attention to its organizational development (OD). Mandatory school district reorganization is a related OD consideration. Organizational development is defined in a wide variety of ways; however, in most every definition it relates closely to the movement of an organization from its current state to some future and hopefully more effective state. OD does not refer to a department within the school system but rather an improvement concept that permeates the entire organization.

Organizations with effective organizational development activities are involved deeply with such terms as reengineering, action research, ambidextrous actions, benefits mapping, co-creative learning, competency management, comprehensive reform, decision engineering, downsizing, employee research, executive development, force field analysis, gap analysis, groupthink, integration, knowledge management, navigation, organizational engineering, performance improvement, reinvention, results orientation, social network, strategic mapping, structured design process, total quality management, transparency, workload equity, workplace democracy, and others. Each of these practices serves toward the revolutionary changes needed for reaching education's best of all worlds goal.

Each of the foregoing OD terms is defined briefly in the following section. The vital importance of these organizational behaviors/practices is defined due to their paramount importance in serving each educational organization's search and accomplish its goals of being its very best. They represent the kinds of thinking and practice that can be utilized toward realizing the best of the world educational results. Question: How many of these terms are in place and active in the school environment in which you work or are most familiar?

> *Reengineering*: focuses on the analysis and design of workflows and business processes within the organization. It helps the organization to rethink how they will work in order to improve services.

Action research: the research administered by one or more teachers in a classroom setting for evaluating and assessing the results of an activity or method of instruction. The research is done and benefitted by the individual person or group conducting it.

Ambidextrous organization: refers to an organization's ability to recognize the contributions of its workers to the overall success of the goals and purposes set forth.

Benefits mapping: focuses on why the program change is necessary. It serves to clarify program priorities and makes planning strategically focused.

Co-creative learning: involves training in new ways of thinking about present practices and ongoing changes that school members must contend.

Competency management: used to map the skill sets required in a position to be certain that the school needs are being met and the purposes of the school's programs are being achieved.

Competency modeling: the process of analyzing and describing types of ranges of abilities, knowledge, and skills present in an organization.

Comprehensive reform: centers on doing away with a reliance on past and/or present rigidity defined policies, relationships, and structures and replacing them with practices that permit cooperative and creative collaboration on the part of diversified communities.

Decision engineering: a framework that unifies a number of the best practices for organizational decision making.

Downsizing: a reduction of personnel, program activities, and other resources toward the purpose of gaining organizational effectiveness or meeting the forced changes being faced due to such factors as economic downturns, population losses, or other program changes resulting from internal and/or external scans of the school-community.

Employee research: the process of collecting and using employee data for beneficial purposes such as helping to increase organizational production.

Executive development: centers on the importance of continuous learning on the part of organizational leaders and the need for updating one's knowledge through the process of continuous learning and reverse mentoring strategies.

Force field analysis: associated with efforts to convince organizational members that the present status is not doing the best for the organization or its members.

Gap analysis: realizing that current performance is not satisfactory, listing the characteristics of the present situation, giving serious consideration toward improvement, listing characteristics or factors needed to achieve the future objectives, and learning about the best practices and processes for filling the gaps.

Groupthink: the concept that believes that group decisions are most promising for continued success.

Integration: consists of the alignment and integration between strategic, social, and technical components by effective collaboration between people with different skill sets. Focus on structural and technical components of change is essential.

Knowledge management: the ways in which organizational leaders take special means for keeping abreast of new research and best practice information for application in the practices of the organization. Such procedures require school leaders to serve as receivers, dispensers, and utilizers of new information and strategies that serve to improve the effectiveness of the organization.

Navigation: the process of managing change through ongoing adaptation. Management changes within the organization, market changes, organizational factors, and others must be balanced while ensuring employee involvement and flexibility in work responsibilities.

Organizational engineering: the science that designs, improves, inspires, implements, and operates an organization through the use of engineering and analysis methods with the objective of efficiency.

Performance improvement: centers on the overall improvement of the major factors of student academic performance and the positive program improvements witnessed by the changes implemented by the school. Hard performance data are relevant here to determine if improvements were actually demonstrated.

Reinvention: based on the concept of continually examining, studying, responding, innovating, reimagining, and adapting to the world around us.

Social network analysis: uses network and graphic theories to investigate social structures within the school-community.

Strategic mapping: a strategic internal communication tool in the form of a diagram that is used to capture how the strategic goals are being pursued by the organization.

Structured design process: focuses on helping school system become more effective by implementing effective interventions that contend with school culture, processes, and structure in order to improve the school system's performance.

Total quality management: consists of efforts to install and make permanent a climate in which an organization can continually improve its effectiveness.

Transparency: describes the openness and availability of communications channels within the organization.

Workload equity: focuses on the fairness of work assignments among employee personnel including teachers and support staff members. Workload assignments can be objectively measured and assessed. However, this is not to infer that all teachers with the same teaching experience or having different teaching assignments should be receiving the same compensation.

Education Inhibitor #7
The Lack of an Effective Research Component within Education Generally and within School Districts Specifically

The issue/problem of research has been discussed in the previous chapters with emphasis on the need to implement viable education research units within the federal, state, and local levels, as well as in the various educational associations and councils across the nation. In chapter 2, recommendations included the establishment of high-quality research components in each state, major improvements for developing research knowledge and skills in educator preparation programs, action research activities in every teacher's classroom, and the contention that much improved, effective educational research is the sine quo non of the best of the world's education ability to actually become the best of all worlds.

Suppose we subtracted all of the medical research that has been accomplished within the past four decades, including the discovery for the vaccination for polio, all of the technological research that served to make a trip to and back from the moon, the myriad of prescription drugs that have saved and increased the life span of thousands of human beings, driverless cars, wireless technology, and on and on. Question, what highly significant educational research has served toward the improvement of education in America that has placed us on or near the top of being the best of all worlds?

Key Chapter Ideas and Recommendations

- Public schools are about community, democracy, and civility.

- The positive programs of public schools must be continued and expanded and the negative inhibiting factors must be reimagined toward the goal of revolutionary changes that result in leading education nationally toward the goal of being the best of all worlds.

- Just putting more dollars into present public schools will not automatically improve education but supporting more funding for education for the purposes of preparing, hiring, and retaining high-quality persons is indeed a need of paramount importance.

- New approaches to teacher compensation must be implemented if indeed the goal of being the best of all worlds is to become more than just singing a happy tune.

- In the end, public education produces the quality of "products" that the citizenry is willing to support financially.

- The question as to whether or not education in America is failing is most likely to be answered by focusing on reimagining the many criticisms that are being set forth by the citizenry.

- Words that are seldom mentioned in conversations about the improvement of public school education are that of valid and reliable educational research. No organization can be effective for any long period of time without the foundation that viable research can provide.

- Continuous opportunities for teacher development are vested in the contention that development in the end is self-development.

- Teacher load and class size are terms commonly viewed as being synonymous. In reality, class size is only one factor that constitutes teacher load. Inequities in teacher load within most every school nationally are extreme. Empirical research reveals that the highest workload commonly is carried by new teachers and the most highly qualified teachers (Norton 1959). Thus, the best teachers tend to be so overly burdened that their performance is reduced to a level of mediocrity. Approximately 30 percent of new teachers leave the profession after their first year of service.

- Professional teacher/administrator academies are recommended to replace the present unsatisfactory preparation programs in all too many university programs.

- Although OD has been with us for several decades, internal reports indicate that the positive characteristics of effective OD practices are absent in the schools in which the faculty works. OD is a most important characteristic of the kind of preparation programs that are visualized in the teacher/administrator academies in America.

Discussion Questions

1. Consider one of the issues facing public school education today. Use your magic wand to reimagine major changes that you would make toward the solution of the problems surrounding the chosen issue.

2. Finance is always among the list of major issues/problems facing education historically. Give thought to the compensation recommendations set forth in this chapter, especially the recommendation of placing a much higher beginning salary for teachers by using funds that are now reserved for retirement. Would such a solution be possible? And if so, would it be accepted in the teacher profession? Why or why not?

3. Assume that you have been asked to speak at a meeting of the Rotary Club consisting of members who are primarily the business leaders in the school-community. At the end of your remarks about several issues facing public schools, you open the floor for questions. One member of the audience raises his hand and says, "All we ever hear is regarding more money, more money. We seldom hear about where the money is going and what has been improved." What is your reaction and response to the member's comments?

4. Give thought to the present preparation programs for teacher preparation as you know or have experienced them. Rate them on a scale of 1 (low) to 5 (high) and then take a minute or so to support your response.

5. As the school principal, you are speaking to your school's parent-teacher association on school administrative responsibilities. At the close of your remarks, one parent raises her hand and asks, "You mentioned something about OD and effective administration. Just what is OD and how is it integrated into our school's operation?" Take a moment to write a paragraph that reveals your response to the parent's question.

6. In a class situation, divide the class members into groups of five. Have each group develop a list of factors that tend to inhibit the accomplishment of important educational goals and objectives. Then have each group select one of the factors on their list and set forth reimagining solutions. Have the groups avoid simplistic solutions such as just suggesting that more money is needed. Have them be more specific as to how the recommended solution might best be achieved.

Case Study
It's Their School, Not Mine

Donna Whitfield, the new superintendent of Wymore School District, was in a planning meeting with the members of the school board to explain her vision for implementing her ideas of the school district's vision of the future. She talked about the inevitable occurrence of change and its implications for the work of the Wymore School District. Her vision of the school district in the next five to ten years was stated in a short phrase about what the school district had to do to "become the best educational program in the state."

One of the long-term board members was not sold on what he viewed as a "change order." "Your vision is somewhat different from our traditional board procedures," he stated. "Trying to set up something that is so far away seems rather contentious. I most likely will not even be on the school board five to ten years from now and what are we to say now regarding what the school board might say years from now."

"Yes," agreed Elsie Miller, "what if what we try to do now doesn't work well with a school board and the community way down the road? We don't need any more criticism about our failures. I am not in favor of trying to change things now."

Case Study Discussion Questions

1. Assume the role of Superintendent Whitfield. What might be your response to the opposing opinions of the two school board members? Use your own immediate reactions to the case study situation or take time to review and think about what information in this chapter would serve you well at this point and time. Keep in mind that you are relatively new to the school district and the school board is still making judgments relative to your administrative leadership. If question #1 is appropriate for implementation in a class exercise, let several small student groups prepare a response for report back to the entire class.

REFERENCES

Corso, R. (2018). "The Importance of Public Education." *Nation of Change* (Blog Post), August 25. https://www.nationofchange.org/2016/10/04/importance-public-education/.

Douglass, H. R. (1951). "The 1950 Revision of the Douglass High School Teaching Load Formula." *NASSP Bulletin* 35: 13–24.

Honda, M., and Weingarten, R. (2015). "How We Should Be Funding Public Schools." *The Hill* (blog), November 17. https://thehill.com/blogs/congress-blog/education/260292-how-we-should-be-funding-public-schools-in-the-21st-century.

Hood, J. (1993). "The Failure of American Public Education." FEE Foundation for Economic Education. Atlanta, GA: Author.

Klein. J. (2011). "The Failure of Americna Schools." *The Atlantic*, June 11. https://www.theatlantic.com/magazine/archive/2011/06/the-failure-of-american-schools/308497/.

National Center for Higher Education Management Systems (2015). *Percent of 18–24 Year Olds Enrolled in College*. Boulder, CO: Author.

Norton, M. S. (1959). "Teacher Load in Nebraska High Schools in Cities from 5,000 to 25,000 Population." Dissertation. University of Nebraska.

Norton, M. S. (2008). *Human Resources Administration for Educational Leaders*. Los Angeles, CA: Sage.

Norton, M. S. (2015). *The Changing Landscape of School Leadership: Recalibrating the School Principalship*. Lanham, MD: Rowman & Littlefield.

Norton, M. S., and Bria, S. (1992). "Toward an Equitable Measure of Elementary School Teacher Load." *Record in Educational Administration and Supervision* 13 (1): 62–66.

Shapiro, S., and Brown, C. (2018). *The State of Civics Education*. February 1. Washington, DC: Center for American Progress.

Silverberg K. (2016). "Silverberg: Education Opens Doors to Opportunity, and Minds to Critical Thinking." *Herald-Tribune* (op-ed), December 15. https://www.heraldtribune.com/opinion/20161215/silverberg-education-opens-doors-to-opportunity-and-minds-to-critical-thinking.

Southern Regional Education Board (2001). *Good Principals Are the Key to Successful Schools—Six Strategies to Prepare More Good Principals*. Atlanta, GA: Author.

U.S. Department of Education (2007). "Archived: A 25 Year History of the IDEA." ED website. https://www2.ed.gov/policy/speced/leg/idea/history.html.

Wexler, N. (2018). "Three Things Schools Need to Do If Democracy Is Going to Work." *Forbes*, July 1. https://www.forbes.com/sites/nataliewexler/2018/07/01/three-things-schools-need-to-do-if-democracy-is-going-to-work/#4b632f273960.

About the Author

Dr. M. Scott Norton has served as a secondary school teacher of mathematics, coordinator of curriculum for the Lincoln, Nebraska School District, assistant superintendent for instruction, and superintendent of schools in Salina, Kansas, before joining the University of Nebraska as professor and vice chair of the Department of Educational Administration and Supervision. Later, he served as professor and chair of the Department of Educational Administration and Policy Studies at Arizona State University, where he is currently professor emeritus.

His primary graduate research and instruction areas include curriculum and supervision, teaching methods, governance policy, instructional leadership, educational leadership, human resources administration, the assistant school principalship, research methods, organizational development, and competency-based administration.

He has published widely in national journals in such areas as teaching/instructional methods, curriculum development, organizational climate, instructional leadership, gifted student programs, student retention, and others.

Most recent textbooks authored by Dr. Norton include the following:

Dealing with Change: The Effects of Organizational Development on Contemporary Practices (2018).

Guiding Curriculum Development: The Need to Return to the Local Level (2016).

Teachers with the Magic: Great Teachers Change Students' Lives (2015).

The Principal as a Learning Leader: Motivating Students by Emphasizing Achievement (2013).

The Principal as a Student Advocate: A Guide for Doing What's Best for All Students (2012).

A Guide for Educational Policy Development: Effective Leadership for Policy Development (2017).

Guiding the Human Resources Function: New Issues, New Needs (2017).

The Principal as Human Resources Leader: A Guide to Exemplary Practices for Personnel Administration (2015).

The Legal World of the School Principal: What Leaders Need to Know about School Law (2016).

The Changing Landscape of School Leadership: Recalibrating the School Principalship (2015).

The Whitehouse and Education Through the Years: Presidents' Educational Views and Significant Educational Contribution (2018).

The Politics of Education (2019).

Dr. Norton has received several state and national awards honoring his services and contributions to the field of educational administration from such organizations as the American Association of School Administrators, the University Council for Educational Administration, the Arizona Administrators Association, and the Arizona Educational Research Association; Arizona State University College of Education Dean's Award for excellence in service to the field; President of the ASU College of Education Faculty Association; and the distinguished service award from the Arizona Information Service. He presently is serving as a member of the ASU Emeritus College Council.

Dr. Norton's state and national leadership positions have included service as executive director of the Nebraska Association of School Administrators, a member of the Board of Directors for the Nebraska Congress of Parents and Teachers, president of the Nebraska Council of Teachers of Mathematics, president of the Arizona School Administrators Higher Education Division, member of the Arizona School Administrators Board of Directors, staff associate of the University Council for Educational Administrators, treasurer of the University Council for School Administrators, Nebraska State Representative for the National Association of Secondary School Principals, member of the Board of Editors for the American Association of School Public Relations, and presently a governance council member for the Emeritus College of Arizona State University.

www.ingramcontent.com/pod-product-compliance
Lightning Source LLC
Chambersburg PA
CBHW030117010526
44116CB00005B/290